The 40DAY
Soul Fast
LEADER'S GUIDE

DESTINY IMAGE BOOKS BY DR. CINDY TRIMM

40 Day Soul Fast

40 Days to Discovering the Real You

UPCOMING RELEASES IN THE SOUL FAST SERIES

Reclaim Your Soul

Reclaim Your Health

The 40 DAY *Soul Fast*
LEADER'S GUIDE

Your Journey to Authentic Living

DR. CINDY TRIMM

DESTINY IMAGE₀ PUBLISHERS, INC.
P.O. Box 310, Shippensburg, PA 17257-0310
"Promoting Inspired Lives."

This book and all other Destiny Image, Revival Press, MercyPlace, Fresh Bread, Destiny Image Fiction, and Treasure House books are available at Christian bookstores and distributors worldwide.

For a U.S. bookstore nearest you, call 1-800-722-6774.
For more information on foreign distributors, call 717-532-3040.
Reach us on the Internet: www.destinyimage.com.

ISBN 13 TP: 978-0-7684-4191-8
ISBN 13 Ebook: 978-0-7684-8758-9

For Worldwide Distribution, Printed in the U.S.A.
1 2 3 4 5 6 7 8 / 16 15 14 13 12

Contents

The 40 DAY *Soul Fast*

Group Leader Guidelines

Welcome! If you are reading this, then you are about to begin an amazing journey that will not only transform your life, but the world! This is an eight-week study of the life of the soul, the practice of fasting, and the process of living more authentically. We encourage you to travel on this 40-day journey with a small group from your church, organization, or family. You were not created to journey alone! There is power in community. There is strength in numbers. I challenge you to bring at least 4 friends along with you on your own soul-healing journey to authentic living. When you do, you will be setting a new kind of trend; you will be leading a global transformation, and engaging in an unprecedented movement for the good of humanity.

As you begin this journey, this set of guidelines will help you experience the best 40 days of your life, as well as give you the tools to lead others through this journey to authentic living!

STEPS TO STARTING A 40 DAY
Soul Fast GROUP

CONSIDER THE JOURNEY!

❧ Pray! Ask the Holy Spirit, the *"Spirit of truth,"* as He is called in John 16:13, to give you guidance as you make your plans. This 40-day journey will talk a great deal about resting in your Creator, what that means, and how it can empower you to live more authentically. We are told in Jeremiah, *"Stop at the crossroads and look around. Ask for the old, godly way, and walk in it. Travel its path, and you will find rest for your souls..."* (Jer. 6:16 NLT)

MAP OUT YOUR COURSE!

❧ Determine a meeting location. Keep in mind the number of people who may attend. You will also need audio-visual equipment. The more comfortable the setting, the more people will enjoy being there, and they will spend more time ministering to each other! Smaller groups may work well meeting in homes, larger groups may need a church or community center to accommodate them. Just a word of caution here—the larger the group, the greater your need for co-leaders or assistants. The ideal small group is difficult to judge, however once you get more than 10-12 people, it becomes difficult for each member to feel "heard." If your group is larger than 12 people, consider having 2 or more small group discussion leaders. Break out into smaller discussion groups, each led by an assistant.

❧ Determine the format of your Soul Fast meetings. At this point, also determine the extent of your fast. The purpose of the Soul Fast is to eliminate toxins in your soul, *not* your body. However, because the soul and body are interconnected, what is good for one is good for the other! We encourage you to take this opportunity to cleanse and detox your body as you dedicate yourself to cleansing and detoxifying your soul. If you choose to pursue a physical fast along with the Soul Fast, please read Appendix A: *The 40 Day Soul Fast Handbook*. Prior to any type of physical fasting, individuals should consult with their doctor.

🐾 Once you have established the extent of your fast, set a schedule for your meetings. Some groups like to have a time of fellowship or socializing either before or after the teaching time, where light refreshments are offered. If you are also pursuing a physical fast—be mindful of the foods that your group members may be fasting from! Water flavored with slices of lemon, lime and/or orange, fresh fruit or vegetable juices, as well as herbal and green teas are all good choices, as well as fruit or vegetable trays with hummus or yogurt dips. Be careful not to focus on food however—always keep in mind the purpose is to focus on healing your soul!

🐾 Establish a start date along with a weekly meeting day and time. This eight-week course should be followed consistently and consecutively. Be mindful of the fact that while there are eight weeks of material, most groups will want to meet one last time after completing the 40th day of work to celebrate. The 9th video session could be used in a celebration event. Look far enough ahead on the calendar to account for anything that might interfere. Choose a weeknight, Saturday morning, or Sunday school time at your church depending on the members of your group.

🐾 Advertise! Getting the word out in multiple ways is most effective. Print up flyers, post a sign-up sheet, make announcements in church services or group meetings, set up your own blog or website or post the event on the social media avenue you and your group utilize. A personal invitation is a great way to reach those who might need that little bit of extra encouragement.

🐾 Gather your materials. Each leader will need the *The 40 Day Soul Fast Leader's Guide Kit*, as well as *The 40 Day Soul Fast* book. Additionally, each participant will need a personal copy of both the *40 Day Soul Fast* book and *Participants Guide*. We have found it best for the materials to all be purchased at one time—many booksellers offer discounts on multiple orders, and you are assured that each member will have their materials from the beginning.

STEP FORWARD!

🐾 Arrive at your meeting in *plenty* of time to prepare; frazzled last-minute preparations do not put you in a place of "rest," and your group member will sense your stress! Ensure that all A/V equipment is working properly, and that you have ample supplies for each member. Nametags are a great idea, at least for the first couple of meetings. Icebreaker and introduction activities are also a good idea for the first meeting.

🐾 Pray for your members. As much as possible, make yourself available to them. As each person discovers their authentic self, they will want to share that discovery! You will also need to encourage those who struggle, grow weary, or lose heart. Make sure your members stay committed so they experience the full benefits of soul healing.

🐾 Embrace the transformational journey that you and your fellow members are embarking on to authentic living! Transformation begins within *you!*

🐾 Multiply yourself. Is there someone you know who was not able to attend your group? Help them to initiate their own small group now that you know how effective soul cleansing can be in a group setting!

Thank you for doing your part in creating a global movement! By helping to heal the world one soul at a time, you are impacting culture with God's greatest good.

It's a better world because of you!

GROUP LEADER CHECKLIST

1–2 MONTHS PRIOR

_____ Have you determined a start date?

_____ Have you determined the format, meeting day and time, and weekly meeting schedule?

_____ Have you selected a meeting location (making sure you have adequate space and A/V equipment available)?

_____ Have you advertised? Do you have a sign-up sheet to ensure you order enough materials?

2 WEEKS–1 MONTH PRIOR

_____ Have your ordered materials? You will need a copy of *The 40 Day Soul Fast* and the *Participants Guide* for each participant.

_____ Have you organized your meeting schedule/format?

1–2 WEEKS PRIOR

_____ Have you received all your materials?

_____ Have you reviewed the DVD's and your Leader's Guide to familiarize yourself with the material, and to ensure everything is in order?

_____ Have you planned and organized your refreshments, if you are planning to provide them? Some leaders will handle this themselves, and some leaders find it easier to allow participants to sign up to provide refreshments if they would like to do so.

FIRST MEETING DAY

Plan to arrive *early!* Give yourself extra time to set up the meeting space, double check all A/V equipment and organize your materials. It might be helpful to ask participants to arrive 15 minutes early the first meeting to allow for distribution of materials and any ice-breaker activity you might have planned.

INTRODUCTION

It is my own firm belief that the strength of the soul grows in proportion as you subdue the flesh.—Mohandas Gandhi

Is not this the kind of fasting I have chosen: to loose the chains of injustice and untie the cords of the yoke, to set the oppressed free and break every yoke? (Isaiah 58:6 NIV)

Welcome to *The 40 Day Soul Fast Leader's Guide!* The volume you hold in your hand will accompany you on this eight-week journey. I am on a mission to reconnect you with the true essence of a healthy soul—to lead you to a place in God where your soul can be healed—to reacquaint you with your authentic self. The next 40 days of getting to know the real you are going to be the best 40 days of your life! More importantly, when you learn to live authentically, from a healed, whole soul, no leaks, no punctures, no wounds—free and clear from artificial, socially-modified, cultural toxins—you will not only change your life, you will be poised to change the world.

We have all heard the phrases, "She's a beautiful soul," "Bless your soul," or "He's a mean old soul." These phrases describe our perception of an individual's nature or character. We are all "soul-people," and I believe that strengthening people at the level of their souls—restoring the soul and establishing it as the core and essence of who they really are as self-directed people of value, intelligence, and greatness—will change the world. We must break the false perception that as individuals, what we do does not make a difference in the greater scheme of things. We are as a nation, as a people, nothing more than the sum of our parts. As the giant world-changer, a small man by the name of Mohandas Gandhi, once said, "A nation's culture resides in the hearts and in the soul of its people." We will only be as whole and healed as a country as we are as a people. Oscar Wilde, the famous Irish poet and novelist said, "Ordinary riches can be stolen, real riches cannot. In your soul are infinitely precious things that cannot be taken from you." To reiterate a soul-searching question posed by Jesus, "What does it really profit us if we gain the whole world and lose our souls—the essence of who we really are and what it means to be human?"

If you are here reading this today, I imagine you have asked yourself that same question. For those of you looking to reclaim your soul and recapture the essence of who you really are, you are in the right place. I created this 40-Day Study to guide you step by step, day by day, into a more authentic life. I am so glad you have chosen to join me on this journey to greater mental, emotional, and spiritual health! If you are looking to transform your life, you need look no further! Let the journey begin!

WHAT IS A SOUL FAST?

The purpose of this *40 Day Soul Fast* is to not only bring health and restoration to the souls of individuals, but also to provide a mechanism for all people to learn to live from the inside out—from their authentic, God-nature selves. This Soul Fast is not addressing the issue of what you are eating, but what's eating you. The goal of this 40-day journey is to guide you through the process of discarding useless toxic emotions—self-sabotaging thoughts and viruses of the mind—so that you can fully move into who God created you to be. You will be invited to examine all of your objectives and relationships, any hidden agendas or motives that have governed your subconscious, in order to thrust you onto a new path of achievement and abundance. This journey is about setting you free once and for all to maximize your greatest potential.

The 40 Day Soul Fast takes place over eight weeks. For simplicity's sake, I have taken these eight weeks and divided them evenly so that you can establish a regular routine Monday through Friday, allowing for weekends off so you can focus on family and worship or make up a missed day if necessary.

Put aside time for "me-moments." Give yourself adequate time to focus on nurturing your inner self. Part of the Soul Fast discipline is not allowing everyday distractions to deter you from cultivating the inner life of your soul. It will require disciplined focus, a heightened mindfulness, and keen sensitivity to the Spirit of God.

We will begin our 40-day journey by talking about capacity building. Week one of our eight-week venture focuses on "The Power of 40: Enlarging Your Capacity." This theme is more fully explored in *The 40 Day Soul Fast,* but for the purposes of this study, it ties together the five characteristics you will find in week one. In week two, we will talk about "The Purpose of a Soul Fast: The Self-Leadership Challenge." In week three, we will discuss "The Nature of the Soul: The Essence of You." In week four, we address "The Properties of Thought: You Are What You Think." Week five brings us to "The Importance of Identity: Becoming a Master by Mastering Your Mind." In week six we look at "The Power of Words: Healing the Hole in Your Soul." In week seven, we deal with "The Power of Doing:

God's Chosen Fast." In week eight, we begin wrapping up by "Sealing the Healing: The Cleansing Power of Love." And after we finish our 40 days, we conclude this journey in week nine with "A Celebration!"

The focus of this study is to develop the 40 characteristics of an authentic person. These characteristics tie in with *The 40 Day Soul Fast,* but you can also use this guide by itself as a tool for focused self-exploration. Each day, you will read a meditation about one of the 40 characteristics of an authentic person. Then you will be given several "Action Steps" to consider as you put these characteristics into practice. Use the space provided to write your responses, reflections, meditations, and anything else God places on your heart as you delve into these powerful characteristics of authenticity.

THE SOUL OF THE MATTER

> Be your authentic self. Your authentic self is who you are when you have no fear of judgment or before the world starts pushing you around and telling you who you're supposed to be. Your fictional self is who you are when you have a social mask on to please everyone else. Give yourself permission to be your authentic self. —Dr. Phil McGraw

This *40 Day Soul Fast* is about finding rest and restoration for your soul. When all is well with the souls of humanity, all will be well in the world. When you have peace in your soul, you will bring that peace to bear on the world around you—you will become the change you are hoping to see.

Over the next eight weeks, you will learn and grow and be empowered like never before to maximize your personal potential and break through to greater success.

May we all feel the presence of God each and every day as we *"do our best to enter that rest"* (Heb. 4:11 NLT). And as we take up residence there, may we become more acquainted with our authentic selves and equipped to walk in the light of what we discover.

Let this study be a tool you can use to clear the ground of every obstruction and build a life of obedience into full maturity (see 2 Cor 10:6 MSG)—the fully complete you! Are you ready to begin the best 40 days of your life?

Let the soul journey begin!

> *Beloved, I pray that you may prosper in all things and be in health, just as your soul prospers* (3 John 1:2 NKJV).

You don't have a soul. You are a Soul.—C. S. Lewis

THE POWER OF FORTY

Pray! Ask God to direct each person to the goal that He has for them as they step out into this journey, and for the wisdom to lead.

WELCOME AND INTRODUCTIONS (15-30 MINS)

- Introduce yourself, and allow each participant to briefly introduce themselves and share their reason for joining this journey.

- Discuss the schedule for the meetings, as well as the entire 40-day journey.

- Distribute materials to each participant. Briefly orient the participants to the book and participants guide, explaining the time commitment for each day. Encourage each person to engage fully in this journey—they will get out of it only as much as they invest.

- Go over Appendix A in the Leaders Guide/Participants Guide. If you or your participants will be doing a physical fast in addition to the Soul Fast, please take time to go over the guidelines. Answer questions as you feel comfortable—always encourage your participants to get the approval of their physician before beginning a physical fast.

VIDEO/TEACHING (30 MINS)

DRILLING DOWN (30 MINS)

- Review the weekly plan as discussed in the video—5 days of journal entries, weekends off.

- Ask your participants to identify a goal or prayer request—they may share if comfortable. At this point, also discuss trust, confidentiality, and transparency with your group. Members will need to know that they are in a safe environment—no one will discuss any detail of your discussions outside the meeting times. This will allow members to share more openly.

- Take a good look at your life, environment, habits, and relationships. What are the things that move you closer to your best life? Farther away?

- What do you sense is keeping you from maximizing your potential?

- What keeps you from living more freely and authentically?

- Point out the 24 questions on page 68-69 of the book and page 183-184 in the participant's guide. Encourage participants to answer these questions as they are able.

JOURNEY PLANS FOR THE NEXT WEEK

Point out Day 1–Day 5 in the book and guide. Encourage everyone to participate fully in this journey in order to get the most out of it.

CLOSE IN PRAYER

David says to restore my soul

WEEK ONE
VIDEO LISTENING GUIDE

Healing the wholes in my soul!!

Could things be the way they are because you are the way you are?

What one thing could you change that could change everything?

Living authentically means living <u>inside out</u>, not <u>outside in</u>.

Everything you need to succeed at life was given to you at <u>conception</u>.

*Giving away your personal power to things
undermines who you really are.*

It's not about what you're eating, but what's eating you.

Noah meant

The 40 Day Soul Fast is about <u>resting</u> in who <u>God</u> says you are.

Your soul houses your <u>mind, will, emotions</u>.

*By placing a lid in one area of your life,
you are placing lids on every area.*

There are no limitations except <u>the limitations in your mind</u>.

*You will place a lid on your own life as long as you think it is
someone else's responsibility to make you happy or successful.*

Sometimes the best place to be is up against a wall.

> **History is going to be kind to me, because I plan to write it.**
> **—Winston Churchill**

Revisit things serval times til it sticks

You will resemble those with whom you assemble.

<u>Enabling</u> a person is not the same thing as <u>empowering</u> a person.

Everything we want in life lies just <u>beyond</u> our <u>comfort zone</u>.

Capacity building starts with someone challenging you, or you challenging yourself.

Jamie your gning you peice of the puzzle

What limitation are you going to remove? Be specific! Dr. Trimm used the term "self imposed impotence." Where is the source of that lie?

Removing a limitation : *self inposd*

Rejection means that others can't handle you.

where has we been condiction where did it start.

No longer staying on the surface but we are drilling down into ourselves to becoming more like you.

THE POWER OF FORTY: ENLARGING YOUR CAPACITY

Capacity building by learning to live authentically is what *The 40 Day Soul Fast* is all about. Capacity building, in a way, is also about community building. It's about growing into *"the fullness of God"* as a community (see Eph. 3 and 4).

During week one of *The 40 Day Soul Fast,* we will focus on how to build capacity by *Transforming, Cleansing, Aligning, Preparing,* and *Loosing.* I mention these topics here because they provide the framework for each of the 40 characteristics of an authentic person. However within the pages of this study guide, we will only be focusing on the individual characteristics themselves.

The first characteristic we will highlight is *Awareness*, which relates to the focus of Day One—*Transforming.* Becoming aware of your current position is the first step in any transformation.

Cleansing is crucial to the beginning of any transformation—removing the impurities is necessary to make way for future growth and change. The characteristic of *Godliness* is your standard for cleanliness.

The characteristic of *Truth* is essential to the process of *Aligning* because Truth is what you need to be aligned *with.* We look at truth on this day as we continue to focus on our goal of capacity building.

Preparing takes *Commitment.* Commitment is a vital characteristic to focus on, and you will need to prepare for the rest of this fast by committing yourself to seeing this process through to the end.

Once you have committed, you will need to learn to practice *Patience.* Patience will help you last long enough to see what God is *Loosing* in your life—the manifestation of His truly wonderful plans for you. Rest assured you'll need to have built your capacity to be ready for it!

Awareness

God's Spirit touches our spirits and confirms who we really are (Romans 8:15).

Today, the first day of your journey to a more authentic life, begins with a focus on *awareness*. This is the first of 40 characteristics that define a person who is living authentically—for how can you be truly yourself if you're not aware of who you truly are?

For now, I want you to simply focus on being more self-aware. Without cultivating self-awareness, nothing else you do will move you toward living more authentically. It is the first step you must take in making the adjustments necessary to correct the course of your life.

If you are to grow as a person, you must be aware of what your thoughts are telling you about whom you are now and who you are capable of becoming. You must have an objective understanding of your own mindsets, habits, challenges, strengths, and weaknesses.

We shall not cease from exploration—and the end of all our exploring will be to arrive where we started and know the place for the first time. —T. S. Eliot

ACTION STEPS

🦶 Describe what you believe are some outstanding characteristics about yourself?

Work Hard
compassate

🦶 How have you capitalized on those and harnessed the inherent power of you?

🦶 What more can you do to maximize your unique set of gifts and minimize your own peculiar shortcomings? *Talking to God about it and laying it at the foot of the cross. And Believe it —*

🦶 Take a look at the 24 questions in Appendix B. Take some time to look them over at the beginning of this 40-day journey. You don't have to answer them all right now; return to reflect on them occasionally throughout the Soul Fast process. Insights will come to you along the way. When these questions keep you awake at night and make you listless during the day, set aside time to pray and journal your thoughts until you find the answers.

🦶 Listen carefully to what you hear God's Spirit saying—that still, small voice—and write down what you hear.

Therefore if any person is [ingrafted] in Christ (the Messiah) he is a new creation (a new creature altogether); the old [previous moral and spiritual condition] has passed away. Behold, the fresh and new has come (2 Corinthians 5:17 AMP).

GODLINESS

God Honoring Life
God likeness

We're being shown how to turn our backs on a godless, indulgent life, and how to take on a God-filled, God-honoring life. This new life is starting right now, and is whetting our appetites for the glorious day when our great God and Savior, Jesus Christ, appears. He offered Himself as a sacrifice to free us from a dark, rebellious life into this good, pure life, making us a people He can be proud of, energetic in goodness (Titus 2:12-14).

As we move through day two of our 40-day Soul Fast, I want to talk to you about the second characteristic of an authentic person: *Godliness*. Godliness begins with the "God-likeness" of your thoughts—the thoughts that govern your mind. It begins by putting on the mind of Christ.

As Paul wrote the Corinthians, *"Examine your motives, test your heart!"* (1 Cor. 11:27). Make sure everything you say, do, think, and choose is lined up with who it is you truly want to be. Check your heart. Clean house by sweeping up any impure motives or stray intentions. Pay attention to how the things you harbor within your heart affect your words and behaviors—and equally important, how your words, habits, and behaviors affect the life of your soul.

I encourage you today to do a thorough study of the word *godliness* and meditate on all it implies. Then ask yourself where you are falling short of it. Eliminate those things that are not "adding to your faith" and supplement those key things Peter listed that will *"have your life on a firm footing"* (2 Pet. 1:10)!

True godliness does not turn men out of the world, but enables them to live better in it and excites their endeavors to mend it. —William Penn

Look up the word Godliness + meditate on it.

ACTION STEPS

🦶 Meditate on the following and journal what you believe the Bible is saying about you as a person: God created human beings in His own image—reflecting His own nature. He blessed them saying: *"Prosper! Reproduce! Fill Earth! Take charge!"* (See Genesis 1:26-28.)

sample

🦶 Sometimes we are our own worst enemy. Are you sabotaging your own success by the thoughts you think? Are you allowing those thoughts to interfere with how God wants you to view yourself? Are you giving someone else permission to lay things on you that aren't yours to carry and don't further you toward your destiny? *Yes*

🦶 Are your past failures holding dominion over your future? Are relationships distracting you, or worse, suppressing your God-like nature for greatness, significance, and love? *Yes*

🦶 In what areas are you living "a godless, indulgent life" and how can you—starting right now—begin living a more "God-filled, God-honoring life?" *Eating lack of commitment Going to Church talking w/ him more about my life*

🦶 What undermining habits do you want God to help you to give up? List them and commit them to prayer. From this day onward, expect God to empower you to live a godly life pleasing to Him.

Pray About ☆ *Hiding from people losing my Joy Don't think much of myself*

Think of your sufferings as a weaning from that old sinful habit of always expecting to get your own way. Then you'll be able to live out your days free to pursue what God wants instead of being tyrannized by what you want (1 Peter 4:1-2).

The way to be truly happy is to be truly human, and the way to be truly human is to be truly godly. —J. J. Packer

TRUTH

Truth demands Honesty

You with open minds; truth-ready minds will see it at once. Prefer my life-disciplines over chasing after money, and God-knowledge over a lucrative career. For Wisdom is better than all the trappings of wealth; nothing you could wish for holds a candle to her (Proverbs 8:9-11).

As we progress on our journey toward authenticity, we have talked about being more self-aware and about the importance of pursuing godliness. To help us do both more fully, we must be willing to take an honest look at our lives and be willing to seek the truth about who we are now versus who God calls us to be in Christ.

The concept of truth has always been at the center of great debates among theologians and scientists. The foundational key to living authentically *is* truth. When truth is absent from our lives, it is impossible for the soul to be truly free. It is, therefore, a spiritual imperative that you should not only be true to yourself, but should continuously strive to live in the full light of the truth and to be governed by the Spirit of Truth. As the psalmist wrote, *"What you're after is truth from the inside out. Enter me, then; conceive a new, true life"* (Ps. 51:6).

Truth demands honesty. Those daring to live authentically must, first and foremost, be honest with themselves and others. Always speak the truth. Exemplify truth. Uphold the truth. Stand on the truth. *Live the truth!*

> Leaders of the future will have the courage to align with principles and go against the grain of old assumptions or paradigms. It takes tremendous courage and stamina to say, "I'm going to align my personal value system, my lifestyle, my direction, and my habits with timeless principles." —Stephen Covey

ACTION STEPS

- Sit quietly with the Spirit of Truth and allow Him to guide you into all truth about who God has created you to be. (See John 16:13.)

But when he, the Spirit of truth, comes, he will guide you into all truth. He will not speak on his own; he will speak only what he hears, and he will tell you what is yet to come.

- Invite the Holy Spirit to reveal "deep and hidden things" about yourself that you should either embrace or change. (See Daniel 2:22 NIV.)

He reveals deep and hidden things; he knows what lies in darkness, and light dwells with him.

- Ask Him to help you filter through what is not of the truth, to cut anything away from your heart or mind that is not true, and to help you cultivate those things that lead *"to finding yourself, your true self"* (Luke 9:23).

Then he said to them all: If anyone would come after me, he must deny himself and take up the cross daily and follow me.

- What would this new, true life look like if it were conceived in you?

I would put Christ first above all else! Deny myself so I could learn to love as he does.

- How can you realign your life so that it reflects the authentic you God had in mind? *I'm praying about this*

When the Spirit of truth comes, He will guide you into all truth. He will not speak on His own but will tell you what He has heard (John 16:13 NLT).

The truth is incontrovertible. Malice may attack it, ignorance may deride it, but in the end, there it is. —Winston Churchill

Day Four

COMMITMENT

Self-sacrifice is the way, My way, to saving yourself, your true self. What good would it do to get everything you want and lose you, the real you? What could you ever trade your soul for? (Mark 8:35-37)

nothing

The difference between those who win at life and those who lose is not based on the amount of education one acquires, the amount of money one earns, nor the superior skills one was born with, but instead is based upon one's level of commitment. Commitment requires faith. You must not only have faith in God, but faith in the person that God has made you to be. That faith will be tested along the way.

The testing and trying of your faith, the refining of your intentions and resolve, the dedication, determination, and perseverance required to stick with something until you've obtained the desired outcome will empower and liberate you—and expand your capacity to do even more. Jesus told His disciples, *"By your steadfastness and patient endurance you shall win the true life of your souls"* (Luke 21:19 AMP).

If you are reading this, you have already demonstrated this characteristic and are well on your way to living truer to your authentic self. Continue to cultivate commitment by sticking with this 40-day endeavor to the very end! It is this steadfast endurance that will strengthen and purify your soul like nothing else.

> A little more persistence, a little more effort, and what seemed hopeless failure may turn to glorious success. —Elbert Hubbard

Day Four

ACTION STEPS

- In light of "thinking bigger," what would your life look like if you were to actually "win the true life of your soul?" Imagine it now.

  I would be confident in who I was
  I would be busy helping others
  I would be going full bore for Christ

- What are you going to commit to doing in order to save the real you?

  Stick to this study
  Keep praying for healing

- Identify one thing you should purge from your life that is causing you to lose the real you.

  Negative Thinking & Talking

- Now identify one thing you could add that will help cultivate your truest self. *Talking + praying that the Lord will give me his strenght*

Staying with it—that's what is required. Stay with it to the end. You won't be sorry (Luke 21:19).

PATIENCE

We continue to shout our praise even when we're hemmed in with troubles, because we know how troubles can develop passionate patience in us, and how that patience in turn forges the tempered steel of virtue, keeping us alert for whatever God will do next (Romans 5:3-4).

Yesterday we talked about commitment. Once you've committed to an endeavor, you will need patience to see it through to completion.

Patience will refine and perfect you. Patience is a discipline you must practice if you want to break free from the myriad of things that can plague and pollute your soul!

Jesus said that it is only by exercising patience that you will learn to *"possess your soul"* (Luke 21:19 NKJV). As you draw closer to your authentic self, you must learn to take possession of your soul by mastering the art of patience.

Developing patience is key to growing into your authentic self and fulfilling your best destiny: *"For you have need of steadfast patience and endurance, so that you may perform and fully accomplish the will of God"* (Heb. 10:36 AMP).

If one advances confidently in the direction of his dreams and endeavors to live the life which he has imagined, he will meet with a success unexpected in common hours. —Henry David Thoreau

ACTION STEPS

🦶 What typically causes you to lose your patience?

Lck of interest

🦶 How can you change your perspective to tap into the power of patience?

Having a stronger relationship with God

🦶 Visualize yourself exercising patient restraint the next time you want to react otherwise.

Let patience have its perfect work, that you may be perfect and complete, lacking nothing (James 1:4 NKJV).

The Purpose of a Soul Fast

Pray! Ask the Holy Spirit for guidance and wisdom as you seek to understand the purpose of a Soul Fast.

Review Your Steps (15 mins)

Review the first week. Encourage members to share observations, comments, or ask questions.

Video/Teaching (30 mins)

Drilling Down (30 mins)

- What are the major events or decisions–or lack thereof–that brought you to where you are now? What is the fruit (rotting, perhaps!) you are carrying with you as a result? Be sensitive to areas of regret or shame that may surface.

- What have you chosen to believe about yourself and others? How is that reflected in your relationships?

- Think on this: the speed at which you choose to believe a thought is how quickly you change the course of your destiny. Your life is simply a representation of the sum total of your choices, choices that either enslave or save your soul. Ultimately, you are only one decision away from changing everything! How does this make you feel? Encouraged?

- Purpose to do this–from here forward, make the decision to align everything you say or do with the Word of God. What do you think will change as a result of this one decision?

Journey Plans for the Next Week

Point out Day 6–Day 10 in the book and guide. Encourage everyone to participate fully in this journey in order to get the most out of it.

Close with Prayer

WEEK TWO
VIDEO LISTENING GUIDE

Heal the soul—heal <u>families</u>, <u>communities</u>, <u>governments</u>.

We seek God's face not just to hear Him talk about <u>Himself</u>, but so that we can hear Him talk about <u>us</u>!

The more you know about <u>God</u>, the more you know about <u>yourself</u>.

What you focus on fuels your <u>thoughts</u>, and whatever fuels your thoughts determines your <u>future</u>.

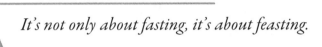

It's not only about fasting, it's about feasting.

Connecting for capacity is not just the capacity for where we're going, but to embrace and love where we came from, because that's why we are the way we are.

You cannot impact people and be the leader you should be if you cannot lead <u>yourself</u>.

What's your skeleton? What do you need to pronounce a benediction on?

*In "being" you will **do**, but in "doing" you won't have the **capacity** to **be**.*

What scaffolding are you using to prop up your life?

No matter how good or bad a situation, to give something up there is a grieving process.

There is only one part of this universe that you can guarantee changing, and that's yourself.

Wholeness requires you to accept responsibility for what you choose to let inhabit your heart.

You are only one decision away from being where you want to be!

Where do you want to be?

Who or what have you allowed to steal your peace?

If it's not paying rent—kick it out!

The Purpose of a Soul Fast: The Self-Leadership Challenge

Fasting is about restraining your natural pleasures and breaking the cycle of stressful living by taking the time to seek God's face, the only One who sees your heart and knows who the authentic you really is. God has the power to break through the clutter that masks your identity, distracts your focus, and keeps you from the abundant life that Jesus died to provide. Your focus areas in developing the self-leadership to accomplish this Soul Fast are *Connecting, Healing, Empowering, Directing,* and *Seeing.*

The purpose of fasting is to reconnect with God, allowing Him to set you free of those things that weigh you down. *Connecting* with God increases your *Capacity!*

Fasting allows the Holy Spirit to reshape you into your true self by dealing with your wounds from the past that have distorted, stagnated, and stunted your essence. As you work through your *Healing,* you are moving toward the characteristic of *Wholeness.*

As you seek God's *Empowering* in order to reach your full capacity, it is very important to focus on *Balance.* This keeps you from seeking power for selfish purposes and allows you to dedicate the gifts of God back to His service.

During this Soul Fast, you will discover an increased ability to discern and follow God's direction. The more you are able to practice *Directing* to bring your ways into alignment with His, the more *Peace* you will have in your life.

Practicing the skill of *Seeing* will allow you to discover the possibilities God wants to show you in unexpected places. What will you see? His *Goodness* becoming real to you.

Day Six

CAPACITY

The unspiritual self, just as it is by nature, can't receive the gifts of God's Spirit. There's no capacity for them (1 Corinthians 2:14).

All human beings are born with capacity. Among the many things we have capacity for is the capacity to grow, to learn, to love, to create, to change, to modify our behavior based on the demands of the situation or circumstance, to succeed, and to prosper. The purpose of *The 40 Day Soul Fast* is to create in you the capacity to hear and receive God's best plan for your life–to enlarge the capacity of your soul for the great work that lies ahead of us all. May you be among those, as Jesus said, *"to whom* [the capacity to receive] *it has been given"* (Matt. 19:11 AMP).

Take time to reflect on what you are hearing the Lord say this week. Press in and focus on discerning the Lord's voice amidst all the static and clutter around you. Clear the ground wherever you are by making room for the presence of God—let Him come and burn up the overgrowth and chaff in your life.

Every day of this 40-day Soul Fast you should be growing more spiritually alive! You should be increasing your capacity to access everything God's Spirit is doing!

Where the spirit does not work with the hand there is no art.
—Leonardo da Vinci

ACTION STEPS

🐾 What have you learned about yourself so far?

🐾 What are four things you will purpose to eliminate?

🐾 What four new habits will you focus on cultivating?

Make the most of what God gives, both the bounty and the capacity to enjoy it, accepting what's given and delighting in the work (Ecclesiastes 5:19).

WHOLENESS

Instead of worrying, pray. Let petitions and praises shape your worries into prayers, letting God know your concerns. Before you know it, a sense of God's wholeness, everything coming together for good, will come and settle you down. It's wonderful what happens when Christ displaces worry at the center of your life (Philippians 4:6-7).

When I pause to consider the course of my life, I conclude that it was divinely orchestrated to bring me to a place of wholeness. Denying, rejecting, judging, or hiding from any aspect of your total being creates pain and results in a lack of wholeness. You cannot adjust what you are not prepared to address.

You are the sum total of all your experiences—good and bad. Wholeness represents a total integration of every facet of your life's experiences. It is the only way to live with congruency, interconnectedness, and completeness.

You can only be complete if your heart is not divided between blame and acceptance. Wholeness requires you to accept responsibility for what you choose to let inhabit your heart.

The one quality that authentic people have is their willingness to take responsibility for their life. When you allow faith and forgiveness to liberate and heal your soul, you will be well on your way to living on the summit of wholeness.

Allow God's Spirit to bring healing to your heart, wholeness to your soul, and that degree of completion we all long for. Paul told the Colossians, *"You are complete in Him"* (Col. 2:10 NKJV).

Nothing can cure the soul but the senses, just as nothing can cure the senses but the soul. —Oscar Wilde

ACTION STEPS

🦶 Identify your most pressing concerns. What causes you to lie awake at night and worry? What distracts you and causes you to furrow your brow throughout the day? Who or what have you allowed to steal your peace?

🦶 Make a commitment to yourself to never wish things did not happen. Accept, learn, and grow from every experience.

🦶 Take responsibility by shaping every irritation, offense, anxiety, or doubt into a prayer. Write down what you notice happens as a result. Who are you able to forgive? How will this affect your network of relationships?

May God Himself, the God who makes everything holy and whole, make you holy and whole, put you together—spirit, soul, and body—and keep you fit for the coming of our Master, Jesus Christ (1 Thessalonians 5:23).

BALANCE

For he who has once entered [God's] rest also has ceased from [the weariness and pain] of human labors (Hebrews 4:10 AMP).

One of the primary reasons for pursuing a Soul Fast is to regain balance in life. What is life balance? It can be hard to describe exactly. A balanced life will look different to different people. But I'm sure we would all agree what it feels like when your life is out of balance! I believe that is why many of you are on this Soul Fast journey. You are seeking balance.

A balanced life is about prioritizing the many activities and responsibilities involved in living—work, home, health, parenting, finances, marriage, etc.—and framing them in such a way that you do not lose touch with yourself in the process. And then, when life throws you a curveball, you are still able to hit a homerun.

Creating balance requires taking a deep breath and finding time in an otherwise busy schedule to nurture yourself and others. Balance is not only about prioritizing what you do, but is also about getting adequate rest. As with wholeness, this comes when you put your entire life into God's hands and allow Him to lead. When your priorities are right, you will feel less stressed and more blessed.

Gaining balance for me began by seeking the Kingdom of God and making His will a priority (see Matt. 6:33). If whatever you do is done "as unto the Lord"—with a grateful heart—not seeking anything but to please God, you will find your life naturally lining up with God's perfect will and infused by His perfect peace

If you are first and foremost honoring God with your every thought and deed, then His peace, joy, and rest will always be near at hand. Remember, this is God's will concerning you!

> Opening your whole being to be an instrument and voice from God, takes something from you as you allow God to work through you, pouring yourself out; empowerment from the Spirit is a rhythm of work and rest.
> —Marlaena Cochran

ACTION STEPS

This week, I encourage you to read Hebrews 4:1-11.

🦶 How does it feel to rest in God?

🦶 What do you need to change in your daily routine to bring true balance?

Bless the Lord, oh my soul, and forget not all His benefits: who forgives all your iniquities, who heals all your diseases, who redeems your life from destruction, who crowns you with loving kindness and tender mercies, who satisfies your mouth with good things, so that your youth is renewed like the eagle's (Psalms 103:2-5 NKJV).

Day Nine

PEACE

Whoever wants to embrace life and see the day fill up with good, here's what you do: Say nothing evil or hurtful; snub evil and cultivate good; run after peace for all you're worth. God looks on all this with approval…but He turns His back on those who do evil things (1 Peter 3:10-12).

If a state of peace is essential for health and prosperity to flourish in a nation, how much more in our individual lives? For this reason Paul told Timothy to pray for *"all who are in authority so that we can live peaceful and quiet lives marked by godliness and dignity"* (1 Tim. 2:2 NLT).

This week practice peace: *"Let the peace of Christ rule in your hearts, since as members of one body you were called to peace"* (Col. 3:15 NIV). How do you practice peace? How do you let the peace of Christ rule in your heart? I leave you with these instructions given by the apostle Peter:

> *Summing up: Be agreeable, be sympathetic, be loving, be compassionate, be humble. That goes for all of you, no exceptions. No retaliation. No sharp-tongued sarcasm. Instead, bless—that's your job, to bless. You'll be a blessing and also get a blessing* (1 Peter 3:8-9).

If there is light in the soul, there will be beauty in the person. If there is beauty in the person, there will be harmony in the house. If there is harmony in the house, there will be order in the nation. If there is order in the nation, there will be peace in the world. —Chinese Proverb

ACTION STEPS

🦶 Mohandas Gandhi said, "Each one of us has to find his peace from within. And peace to be real must be unaffected by outside circumstances." Jesus said, *"Let not your heart be troubled"* (John 14:1 NKJV). Think of some practical things you can do in your life today to manifest peace.

🦶 Focus on allowing the peace of Christ to rule in your heart. When Christ's peace rules your inner world, how will that affect your outer world?

🦶 Be willing to let go of whatever does not produce peace. Pray, and write down anything the Spirit brings to your mind.

This core holy people will not do wrong. They won't lie, won't use words to flatter or seduce. Content with who they are and where they are, unanxious, they'll live at peace (Zephaniah 3:12-13).

Day Ten

GOODNESS

Each person has inside a basic decency and goodness. If he listens
to it and acts on it, he is giving a great deal of what it is the world
needs most. It is not complicated but it takes courage. It takes
courage for a person to listen to his own goodness and act on it.
—Pablo Casals

Paul posed one of the most compelling questions when he challenged the Romans:

*You surely don't think much of God's wonderful goodness or of His patience and
willingness to put up with you. Don't you know that the reason God is good to
you is because He wants you to turn to Him?* (Romans 2:4 CEV)

It is the goodness of God that leads to repentance. It is only because of God's goodness
that we can have any hope of being good ourselves.

One of the most detoxifying things you can do for your soul is to turn to God and
repent. When you turn away from thoughts and habits that are contrary to the Spirit of
Christ, and instead turn toward God and His ways, you become "rich in goodness." As
Paul told the Romans: *"You yourselves are rich in goodness, amply filled with all [spiritual]
knowledge"* (Rom. 15:14 AMP).

Get reacquainted with your authentic self. Determine to be filled with God's goodness,
and to express it.

After the knowledge of, and obedience to, the will of God, the next aim must
be to know something of His attributes of wisdom, power, and goodness as
evidenced by His handiwork. —James Prescott Joule

ACTION STEPS

🦶 Examine your life, your habits, your heart, and your thoughts: Are they an expression of the life of Christ in you, "rich in goodness"?

🦶 How might these things be different if they consisted of "every form of goodness"?

🦶 Think of one negative thing you can replace with something positive.

For the fruit…of the Light or the Spirit [consists] in every form of kindly goodness, uprightness of heart, and trueness of life (Eph. 5:9 AMP).

THE NATURE OF THE SOUL

Pray! Ask Creator God for wisdom as you seek to understand the nature of the Soul.

REVIEW YOUR STEPS (15 MINS)

Review the second week. Encourage members to share observations, comments, or ask questions.

VIDEO/TEACHING (30 MINS)

DRILLING DOWN (30 MINS)

- Look up Isaiah 58:6 and Galatians 5:1—have a volunteer read each passage aloud.

- What you allow to govern your soul is what you permit to occupy it. Do you agree with this?

- Is your soul governed by the love of *things*, or the love of God?

- What do you spend the most time thinking about?

- What do you most hope and long for—in general? For this Soul Fast?

- How can you be a child of God and still a slave to sin?

- What are the toxins and ties contaminating and entangling your soul, keeping it vulnerable to sin and cycles of failure?

JOURNEY PLANS FOR THE NEXT WEEK

Point out Day 11–Day 15 in the book and guide. Encourage everyone to participate fully in this journey in order to get the most out of it.

CLOSE IN PRAYER

Allow time for personal prayer requests.

Week Three
Video Listening Guide

How can you do what you do in such a simple way that the whole world says "that's true elegance"?

> *Is not this the kind of fasting I have chosen: to loose the chains of injustice and untie the cords of the yoke, to set the oppressed free and break every yoke?* (Isaiah 58:6 NIV)

> *It is for freedom that Christ has set us free. Stand firm, then, and do not let yourselves be burdened again by a yoke of slavery* (Galatians 5:1).

Your soul can be _____ various answers _____

You don't have a soul, you are a soul.

Nephish (Greek)—breathing, thinking, being, a complete living being.

Spirit makes you God-conscious.

Body makes you world-conscious.

Soul makes you self-conscious; it is the ability to say that you are separate from others.

The soul is _____ (lots of differents answers possible) _____.

Soul houses mind, will, emotions, seat of your consciousness, intelligence, reason.

To ignore your soul is to ignore yourself.

You are not the roles that you play.

You cannot turn to the <u>created</u> to determine who you are, you've got to go to the <u>Creator</u>!

What is unique about you?

Who really knows you with your mask down?

What's keeping you from finding your unique expression—that one thing that God has put you here to do?

What spin has God placed on your humanity that is so different that you add value to other people?

What really brings you joy?

What are your joy stealers, and how do you deal with them?

THE NATURE OF THE SOUL: THE ESSENCE OF YOU

The soul is that aspect of your whole being that correlates, integrates, and enlivens everything going on in the various dimensions of your self—things like your appetites, ambitions, thoughts, and motivations. It's what makes you, you.

Disaster happens when your soul becomes organized around feelings. A negative feeling or prevailing mood can spread into your whole life; like a red towel in a load of white clothes—it bleeds on everything.

However, God also gave you emotions that would incline you to enjoy participating in life—as well as to turn you away from desires that could keep you in bondage and morph into full-blown lusts.

The key isn't to deny or repress your feelings—but to control them. As you explore the nature of the soul this week, your characteristics of authenticity are connected to the themes of *Becoming, Restoring, Resting, Imaging,* and *Sensing.*

The soul isn't something you have, but rather who you are. *Becoming* your authentic self—your true soul—will take a considerable amount of this day's characteristic—*Discipline.*

The key to *Restoring* your soul is living what you believe in every dimension of your life. This is possible when your life is defined by the characteristic of *Simplicity.*

Resting allows your soul to recharge and connect back to God. The characteristic linked to *Resting* is *Uniqueness.* Take time to rest and thank God for making you uniquely *you.*

Imaging means representing God on this earth—showing the world His image in you—and one of the most powerful ways you can do this is through your unique, God-given *Passion.*

Everyone has feelings and relates to the world largely through *Sensing*—their ability to feel. However, the soul should never be controlled by emotions. Instead, learn to embrace God's *Joy,* which should define your authentic life. When you are characterized by joy, you're living out of who you really are!

Day Eleven

DISCIPLINE

Exercise daily in God—no spiritual flabbiness, please! Workouts in the gymnasium are useful, but a disciplined life in God is far more so, making you fit both today and forever (1 Timothy 4:7-8).

The key to a successful, prosperous life is discipline. Paul emphasized the importance of discipline in almost every letter he wrote. In the Book of Acts he said, *"I always exercise and discipline myself…to have a clear (unshaken, blameless) conscience, void of offense toward God and toward men"* (Acts 24:16 AMP).

Paul wrote Timothy declaring: *"God has not given us a spirit of fear and timidity, but of power, love, and self-discipline"* (2 Tim. 1:7 NLT).

Peter also wrote about discipline: *"So don't lose a minute in building on what you've been given, complementing your basic faith with…alert discipline"* (2 Pet. 1:5).

A disciplined life in God will produce the fruit of the Spirit: *"love, joy, peace, patience, kindness, goodness, faithfulness, gentleness, and self-control"* (Gal. 5:22-23 NLT). Discipline will empower you to become and to do the extraordinary.

Moral excellence comes about as a result of habit. We become just by doing just acts, temperate by doing temperate acts, brave by doing brave acts. —Aristotle

ACTION STEPS

🦶 How do we exercise a disciplined life in God?

🦶 Paul said the discipline of God is not so much about what we choose *not* to do, but more about what we choose *to* do. Make a list of things you can actively choose to do for God.

🦶 Discipline starts in the mind. For every negative thought or negative word you think or speak today, commit to give $1.00 to a charity of your choice.

Get out there and walk—better yet, run—on the road God called you to travel. ...Do this with humility and discipline—not in fits and starts, but steadily, pouring yourselves out for each other in acts of love (Ephesians 4:1-3).

Day Twelve

SIMPLICITY

Here's what I want you to do: Find a quiet, secluded place so you won't be tempted to role-play before God. Just be there as simply and honestly as you can manage. The focus will shift from you to God, and you will begin to sense His grace (Matthew 6:6).

The 40 days of Lent, as with any fast, represents a period of time set aside for keeping the main thing the main thing—for focusing on what is important in our lives as children of God. It's essential that we don't get distracted by "dos" and "don'ts," but remain focused on the power of hoping and believing in Christ as evidenced by our love for one another.

Simplicity does not mean that things are simpler or less demanding. It means that anything superfluous and not needed is discarded and replaced by what is necessary. The Bible states over and over that it is not sacrifice but obedience the Lord seeks—and our love walk demonstrates that obedience. We know we are led of the Spirit when we choose love.

Keep it simple. Walk in love. This is how you will uncover your authentic self, created in the image of love. Just be yourself before God, for God loves you just as you are! And being yourself before Him is how you can love Him in return. Love being yourself.

True religion is real living; living with all one's soul, with all one's goodness and righteousness. —Albert Einstein

ACTION STEPS

🦶 How does the geography of your soul look? Do you need to establish order, repair the power lines, or just mend some fences? Make a list of what these are and begin to address them immediately.

🦶 Today, feed your soul by pursuing the simplicity demonstrated by Christ—demonstrate love. List some practical things you can do to show this.

You have purified your souls in obeying the truth through the Spirit in sincere love of the brethren, love one another fervently with a pure heart (1 Peter 1:22 NKJV).

Uniqueness

You shaped me first inside, then out; You formed me in my mother's womb...body and soul, I am marvelously made! What a creation! You know me inside and out, You know every bone in my body; You know exactly how I was made, bit by bit, how I was sculpted from nothing into something. Like an open book, You watched me grow... the days of my life all prepared before I'd even lived one day (Psalm 139:13-16).

Your soul is what makes you uniquely you. Your soul is imprinted with an eternally unique DNA that holds within it the keys to your purpose, potential, and destiny. I say "eternally unique" because nobody in the history of the world has ever been—or ever will be—just like you.

Today, I want you to stir up the unique expression of God's glory and grace He has woven into your soul—the divine essence of your being. Call out and celebrate those things that make you uniquely you. Be grateful for the gift God created you to be! Rejoice in the wonder and majesty that is you!

To have a firm persuasion in our work—to feel that what we do is right for ourselves and good for the world at the same exact time—is one of the great triumphs of human existence. —David Whyte

ACTION STEPS

Meditate on the following:

Each second we live is a new and unique moment of the universe, a moment that will never be again. And what do we teach our children? We teach them that two and two make four and that Paris is the capital of France. When will we also teach them what they are? We should say to each of them: Do you know what you are? You are a marvel. You are unique. In all the years that have passed, there has never been another child like you. Your legs, your arms, your clever fingers; the way you move. You may become a Shakespeare, a Michelangelo, or a Beethoven. You have the capacity for anything.—Pablo Picasso

If a man does not keep pace with his companions, perhaps it is because he hears a different drummer. Let him step to the music which he hears, however measured or far away. —Henry David Thoreau

🐾 List five aspects of your personality that make you special.

🐾 List five desires that are uniquely yours.

🐾 List five strengths that you bring to the table.

🐾 List five talents that God has given you to steward.

I will praise You, for I am fearfully and wonderfully made; marvelous are Your works, and that my soul knows very well (Psalm 139:14 NKJV).

Passion

God's holy people passionately and faithfully stand their ground (Revelation 13:10).

Yesterday we talked about the importance of embracing your uniqueness. Today I want to talk to you about the importance of embracing your passions. It is passion that gives us eyes to see what is possible, and the fortitude to pursue it. Passion will cause you to take risks and stand against the odds: *"God's holy people passionately and faithfully stand their ground"* (Rev. 13:10).

The things you are passionate about are God-given desires. God's desires in you will move you out of the egocentric, self-centered realm you would otherwise occupy. They cause you to live on a higher plane and tap into the dimension of supernatural ability and resources.

> When work, commitment, and pleasure all become one and you reach that deep well where passion lives, nothing is impossible. —Nancy Coey

ACTION STEPS

🦶 What are you passionate about?

🦶 How can you harness the power of your passions to establish yourself, take dominion, and make a difference within your family, community, or country?

🦶 Your inherent passions are part of your genetic makeup. How can you tap into your passions to "go and do your best?"

You do so well in so many things—you trust God, you're articulate, you're insightful, you're passionate, you love—now go and do your best (2 Corinthians 8:7).

JOY

May the God of hope fill you with all joy and peace in believing, that you may abound in hope by the power of the Holy Spirit (Romans 15:13 NKJV).

The characteristic of joy—and joyfulness—is one of the most, if not *the* most, significant and telling traits of an authentic person. It demonstrates, as well as determines, successful authentic living in so many ways.

Jesus came to empower you to maximize your joy because joy is your key to victory and a more vibrant and satisfying life. Joy is not only healing and restorative, but it is a powerful spiritual force. Jesus sought to teach you how to harness the raw power of simple joy. As the author and finisher of our faith, Jesus tapped into the power of joy to enable Him to endure the Cross (see Heb. 12:2). Now that's powerful.

If the sight of the blue skies fills you with joy, if a blade of grass springing up in the fields has power to move you, if the simple things in nature have a message you understand, rejoice, for your soul is alive. —Eleanora Duse

ACTION STEPS

✔ How can you stir up joy in your everyday life? Be specific.

✔ Discouragement, loss, depression, disappointment, fear, anxiety, oppression, sickness, lack, and loneliness are common joy-thieves. What are some of the things stealing your joy? What will you do to eliminate them?

The joy of the Lord is your strength and stronghold (Nehemiah 8:10 AMP).

THE PROPERTIES OF THOUGHT

Pray! Ask Creator God for wisdom as you seek to understand the thought patterns that rule your soul.

REVIEW YOUR STEPS (15 MINS)

Review the third week. Encourage members to share observations, comments, or ask questions.

VIDEO/TEACHING (30 MINS)

DRILLING DOWN (30 MINS)

- "Winning the battle in your thought life requires daily meditation on the truths found in Scripture, studying the Word of God, and becoming an earnest and lifelong student of the art of spiritual warfare." Does this line up with your current belief system? Have you experienced spiritual warfare?

- Every battle is won or lost in the arena of your mind. How can you prepare for these battles? What weapons have we been given? What is your training regimen?

- What are your thoughts on your current 'thoughts'?

- How have you experienced 'thinking for a change'?

- Read Philippians 4:8 aloud! Encourage participants to commit this verse to memory!

JOURNEY PLANS FOR THE NEXT WEEK

Point out Day 16–Day 20 in the book and journal. Encourage everyone to participate fully in this journey in order to get the most out of it.

CLOSE IN PRAYER

Week Four
Video Listening Guide

Your thoughts brought you to where you are today.

Finally, brothers, whatever is true, whatever is honorable, whatever is just, whatever is pure, whatever is lovely, whatever is commendable, if there is any excellence, if there is anything worthy of praise, think about these things (Philippians 4:8 ESV).

The meaning of a word is always in a <u>person</u>, and we must take <u>responsibility</u> for how we interpret it.

Are you prepared to take responsibility for what goes on in your thought life?

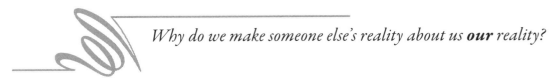

*Why do we make someone else's reality about us **our** reality?*

The quality of your <u>thoughts</u> and the quality of your <u>reality</u> are inextricably related.

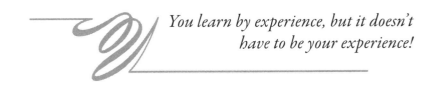

You learn by experience, but it doesn't have to be your experience!

Your <u>imagination</u> is more powerful than your <u>memory</u>.

For as he thinks in his heart, so is he (Proverbs 23:7 NJKV).

Can you be better than what you are now?

What is your life philosophy?

Ten years from now, who do you see yourself becoming? Harness your thoughts to put yourself where you see yourself!

words will produce *thinking*

thinking will produce *emotions/feelings*

feelings will produce *decisions*

decisions will produce *actions*

actions will produce *habits*

habits will produce *character*

character will bring you to your *destiny*

Creflo Dollar

THE PROPERTIES OF THOUGHT: YOU ARE WHAT YOU THINK

There is scientifically measurable power to your thoughts. Your thoughts are all of the ways you are conscious of reality—they form your reality—your memories, beliefs, ideas, and images. Most of these ways of knowing reside so deeply in you that it is hard to tell which may be affecting your life. You will never have more, or go farther, or accomplish greater things than your thoughts will allow. But as quickly as light illuminates a room, a single thought can shed new light on your life, changing everything including your destiny. Changing your thinking is about *Believing, Receiving, Focusing, Envisioning,* and *Conquering.*

One of the most compelling reasons for journeying toward authenticity is to uncover the genuine beauty of your truest self. *Believing* in that *Beauty* makes it a fact in your mind, and your thoughts determine your reality.

Receiving messages from God can happen when you embrace the characteristic of *Effortlessness*—not striving, conniving, manipulating, or clamoring to get ahead, but just *being* and letting God speak to you.

Focusing your mind is like setting the sails on a sailboat. Bring all your thinking to one focus—*Authenticity.* Living out of your truest self—who God created you to be.

The ability to harness your imagination to picture the possibilities before you is called *Envisioning.* It will take a lot of *Focus* to keep that vision foremost in your mind.

As we conclude our focus on our thought life, remember that you have an enemy out there, and he is attacking your thoughts. Set yourself on *Conquering* the enemy's tactics. To do this you must exhibit the characteristic of *Order.* An ordered life allows you to keep your focus set, in spite of the attacks that try to sway you, and keep your thought life determined by authenticity.

Day Sixteen

BEAUTY

If God gives such attention to the appearance of wildflowers—most of which are never even seen—don't you think He'll attend to you, take pride in you, do His best for you?" (Matthew 6:30)

One of the most compelling reasons for journeying toward authenticity is to uncover the genuine beauty of your truest self. It is a process of peeling away the layers of artificial roles we so often play and the lies and limitations we impose on our own souls.

True beauty comes from within—which lends truth to the statement: "Beauty is as beauty does." Beauty is also in the eye of the beholder. Mohandas Gandhi said, "When I admire the wonders of a sunset or the beauty of the moon, my soul expands in the worship of the creator."

The beauty you see is a result of the beauty emanating from your own soul. Though many say that life is not a bed of roses, I believe that it is. Like a rose, if you judge it by the prick of its thorns and cast it aside as painful, you will miss its beauty. Sometimes people miss beauty because it is uncomfortable or unfamiliar. Try to find the beauty in things and people beyond the obvious.

When I think of cultivating "beauty of soul," I think of a soul's originality, vibrancy, and richness—awe-provoking intricacy and complexity of color—great depths and heights of potential—and the human soul's immense capacity to reflect God's glory.

Your soul is beautiful if for no other reason than it was created to express the divine magnificence of the Creator.

Insomuch as love grows in you, so in you beauty grows. For love is the beauty of the soul. —St. Augustine

ACTION STEPS

🦶 What would it look like to relax and "respond to God's giving"—to simply *"be still and rest in the Lord; wait for Him and patiently lean yourself upon Him; fret not yourself"* (Ps. 37:7 AMP)? What kind of a beauty treatment would that be for your soul?

🦶 Create space in your life for a spiritual beauty spa. Soak in God's presence. Allow God's Spirit to wash away any impurities, to peel away the old, dead things and soften the rough places.

🦶 Stop striving. Stop fussing. Relax in the beautiful you God created you to be and worship Him in that beauty.

Worship the Lord in the beauty of holiness (Psalm 96:9 NKJV).

EFFORTLESSNESS

He energizes those who get tired…those who wait upon God get fresh strength. They spread their wings and soar like eagles, they run and don't get tired; they walk and don't lag behind (Isaiah 40:29-31).

We don't often think of "effortlessness" as a characteristic we should cultivate in our lives. Most of us were raised to always try harder and do more in order to maximize our potential. Although my life mission *is* to empower people to maximize their potential, I believe the key is not in maximizing one's *"doing"* as much as one's *"being."*

When I think of effortlessness, I think of entering God's rest—a major theme throughout the Bible. Living authentically has much to do with living effortlessly—not striving, conniving, manipulating, clamoring to get ahead, etc.

When you rest in God, you are operating from a place of supernatural power, causing everything you do to seem effortless. It may take effort to enter that place, but it will energize you once you're there.

Repose is a quality too many undervalue. In the clamor one is irresistibly drawn to the woman who sits gracefully relaxed, who keeps her hands still, talks in a low voice, and listens with responsive eyes and smiles. She creates a spell around her, charming to the ear, the eye and the mind. —Good House-keeping, November 1947

ACTION STEPS

🦶 Where do you need more "know-how"—or where in your life are you feeling opposition or boxed in? What does *not* feel effortless?

🦶 Try putting effort instead into pursuing God's rest. Practice "being still" and trusting God to lift you up so you soar—no, *vault*—effortlessly over the highest fences.

🦶 Keep company with God so you learn to live freely and lightly.

Walk with Me and work with Me—watch how I do it. Learn the unforced rhythms of grace. I won't lay anything heavy or ill-fitting on you. Keep company with Me and you'll learn to live freely and lightly (Matthew 11:29-30).

Day Eighteen

AUTHENTICITY

Examine yourselves to see if your faith is genuine. Test yourselves
(2 Corinthians 13:5 NLT).

This week we have been talking about the nature of the soul. Your soul is the divine, eternal essence of you. An uncluttered, healed, and whole soul represents your true, authentic self. Learning to living authentically is the purpose of this 40-day journey.

So what is authenticity?

Authenticity simply means being true to who you are—aligning your every thought and action with who and what you were created to be and do.

Judy Garland stated, "Always be a first-rate version of yourself instead of a second-rate version of someone else." Steve Jobs gave the following advice: "Your time is limited, so don't waste it living someone else's life. Don't be trapped by dogma, which is living with the results of other people's thinking. Don't let the noise of other's opinions drown out your own inner voice. And most importantly, have the courage to follow your heart and intuition. They somehow already know what you truly want to become. Everything else is secondary." While Charles Evans Hughes concluded, "When we lose the right to be different, we lose the privilege to be free."

Nothing or no one should define you—it is up to you to understand who you are and live according to that truth.

Take the lead in letting others step to the music they hear by dancing to your own.

> That inner voice has both gentleness and clarity. So to get to authenticity, you really keep going down to the bone, to the honesty, and the inevitability of something. —Meredith Monk

ACTION STEPS

🦶 If God were to drop a plumb line into the building you've created of your life, how aligned would it be with His original blueprint for you? (See Amos 7:7-8.)

🦶 How can you realign your life so that it reflects the authentic you God had in mind?

What good would it do to get everything you want and lose you, the real you? What could you ever trade your soul for? (Mark 8:36-37)

FOCUS

I've got my eye on the goal, where God is beckoning us onward...
I'm off and running, and I'm not turning back...I focus on this one
thing: forgetting the past and looking forward to what lies ahead...I
keep focused on that goal. If any of you have something else in mind,
something less than total commitment, God will clear your blurred
vision—you'll see it yet! Now that we're on the right track, let's stay
on it (Philippians 3:12-16).

The number one thing that keeps people from realizing their goals, maximizing their potential, and fulfilling their purpose is focus. Wherever you place your focus - your mind, talents, abilities, and emotions will follow.

In other words, the life and reality you are experiencing are a reflection of the thoughts you are thinking. This is why you are told in Psalms to *"guard your heart above all else, for it determines the course of your life"* (Prov. 4:23 NLT). Ultimately, the power of our thoughts translates into our ability to focus. It's focused thought that wields the greatest power.

If you do not want to see something in your future, do not focus on it today. Train your mind to focus on the positive, and you will always have positive outcomes.

Our thoughts create our reality—where we put our focus is the direction we tend to go. —Peter McWilliams

ACTION STEPS

🐾 What is God calling you to do? Focus on your calling, not your circumstances.

🐾 What is it you want more of? If you want more of God and His power working in your life, focus on God and His power!

🐾 Focus on what you want, not what you don't want! Do not allow anything or anyone to alter your focus.

Keep your eyes straight ahead; ignore all sideshow distractions. Watch your step, and the road will stretch out smooth before you. Look neither right nor left; leave evil in the dust (Proverbs 4:25-27).

Day Twenty

ORDER

Look carefully then how you walk! Live purposefully and worthily and accurately, not as the unwise and witless, but as wise (sensible, intelligent people), making the very most of the time [buying up each opportunity], because the days are evil. Therefore do not be vague and thoughtless and foolish, but understanding and firmly grasping what the will of the Lord is (Ephesians 5:15-17 AMP).

Yesterday we talked about the power of focus. Sometimes it is a challenge to not only *set* our focus on what we should, but to *keep* our focus once we do. One of the tools—or characteristics—that will help you *stay* focused is learning to order your thoughts.

Nothing will help you keep order in your mind more than establishing order in your daily life. I'm talking about making the most of your time every day and eliminating "time wasters." If your day is cluttered or full of toxic activities, so will be your mind! Junk time is as bad as junk food! Take account of the empty time calories that make up the daily sustenance of your life in the form of television watching, Internet surfing, magazine perusing, or even gossiping with coworkers. As Paul told the Ephesians, *"Don't live carelessly, unthinkingly"* (Eph. 5:17)—*"make every minute count"* (Eph. 5:16 CEV).

This is the beginning of a new day. God has given me this day to use as I will. I can waste it or use it for good. What I do today is important, because I am exchanging a day of my life for it. When tomorrow comes, this day will be gone forever, leaving in its place something that I have traded for it. I want it to be gain, not loss; good not evil; success not failure; in order that I shall not regret the price I paid for it. —Author Unknown

ACTION STEPS

🦶 As you sit quietly in the presence of God, take an account of how you spend or allocate each hour of each day, just like you keep an account of how you spend money or allocate calories.

🦶 How can you "reorder" your day to help you better order your thoughts?

🦶 How does the order, or lack of order, in your home, office, car, or garage affect the order, or lack of order, in your soul? Is there room for more order? How will you bring that to pass? When?

Consider well the path of your feet, and let all your ways be established and ordered aright (Proverbs 4:26 AMP).

The Importance of Identity

Pray! Ask Father God for insight as you seek to understand your identity in Christ.

Review Your Steps (15 mins)

Review the fourth week. Encourage members to share observations, comments, or ask questions.

Video/Teaching (30 mins)

Drilling Down (30 mins)

❧ The ultimate key to deliverance in this life is embracing who you are in Christ—and who He is within you. Can you put into words your own identity in Christ?

❧ Whatever has ensnared you is not greater than God's power—and desire—to set you free! Do you believe this?

❧ According to 2 Cor 5:17, anyone who belongs to Christ is a new creation; the old has gone and the new has come! Have you accepted that truth? It is possible to have participants who have not yet accepted Christ as their Savior, or some may feel the need to recommit their lives to God. Offer a time of prayer, with eyes closed, and encourage those who would like to take this step to repeat after you: *Dear God in heaven, I come to you in the name of Jesus. I acknowledge to You that I am a sinner, and I am sorry for my sins and the life that I have lived apart from You. I need your forgiveness. I believe that your only begotten Son Jesus Christ shed His precious blood on the cross at Calvary and died for my sins, and I am now willing to turn from my sin. You said that if we confess Jesus as Lord and believe in our hearts that God raised Him from the dead, we will be saved. Right now I confess Jesus as the Lord of my soul. With my heart, I believe that God raised Jesus from the dead. This very moment I accept Jesus Christ as my own personal Savior and according to His Word, right now I am saved. Thank you for your free gift of salvation. In Jesus' name, amen.* Make special note of anyone who made this decision for the first time and offer them extra encouragement as well as any resources you or your church can provide.

❧ You learn more about who you were created to be by learning about who He is. The more time you spend learning about the nature of God, learning the ways of Christ, and keeping company with His Spirit, the more you are transformed into His likeness. How have you experienced this truth?

🐌 How can you more fully embrace your identity in Christ? What does that look like? How do you walk that out in everyday life?

🐌 How does this knowledge of your true identity enable you to live more authentically?

JOURNEY PLANS FOR THE NEXT WEEK

Point out Day 21–Day 25 in the book and guide. Encourage everyone to participate fully in this journey in order to get the most out of it.

CLOSE IN PRAYER

WEEK FIVE
VIDEO LISTENING GUIDE

What is your definition of identity?

What breadcrumbs, or clues, can you use to discover who you are?

The greatest conversation we can have with God starts with, "Who am I? Who am I called to be?"

Personality is who you are, and it's from God. Temperament is changeable.

You can only adjust what you address.

Identity is boundary of self—it's where I start and stop and where you start and stop.

Identity gives me a clue to my purpose.

When people call your name, what image comes to their mind?

Who am I? Why am I here?

Where am I going? How am I going to get there?

What resources has God left for me?

Who should be going with me?

What kind of legacy am I going to leave?

*The thing that you are pushing **at** is the thing that's eating you.*

I AM...

- God's child (see John 1:12)

- Christ's friend (see John 15:5)

- A member of Christ's Body (see 1 Cor. 12:27)

- A saint, a holy one (see Eph. 1:1)

- Redeemed and forgiven of all my sins (see Col. 1:14)

- Complete in Christ (see Col. 2:10)

- Free from condemnation (see Rom. 8:1-2)

- Assured that all things work together for good (see Rom. 8:28)

- Secure and cannot be separated from the love of God (see Rom. 8:35-39)

- A citizen of Heaven (see Phil. 3:20)

- Given a spirit of power, love and discipline (see 2 Tim. 1:7)

- Chosen and appointed by God to bear fruit (see John 15:16)

- A temple of God (see 1 Cor. 3:16)

- Seated with Christ In the heavenly realm (see Eph. 2:10)

- God's workmanship, created for good works (see Eph. 2:10)

- The apple of His eye (see Deut. 32:9-10)

Why be a poor copy of someone else, when
you can be a very good original?

The Importance of Identity: Becoming a Master by Mastering Your Mind

Who are you really? Have you ever asked yourself that question in earnest? Most of us are so focused on what we do day to day—often struggling to meet the expectations of others—that we don't stop to ask who we are created to be. I am convinced that if we focused more on our character—rather than our career or the company we keep—we would be living more meaningful and impactful lives. We would be able to tap into the unique strengths and creative potential with which we have each been endowed. We would move beyond the cookie-cutter lives that so many have found to be shallow and unfulfilling.

As you focus this week on discovering who you truly are, your five characteristics will be linked to the topics of *Embracing, Agreeing, Capitalizing, Belonging,* and *Becoming.*

As you progress through this fast and begin to discover who God made you to be, you will be faced with the task of *Embracing* your authentic self. In order to do this, the characteristic of *Faith* will help you, keeping you rooted and grounded in authenticity.

When it comes to your value and identity, who are you *Agreeing* with? God says you are fearfully and wonderfully made. When you agree with Him, it prompts you to respond with another powerful characteristic—*Gratitude* for all He has given you.

When you understand who you really are, you can begin *Capitalizing* on your unique strengths and talents. These were given to you by God to specifically equip you for your unique *Destiny.*

Many people struggle today because they lack a sense of *Belonging.* They are lonely because they cannot be themselves around others. When you are living in your true *Identity,* the relationships you have with others will also be more authentic.

Becoming involves a process of growth, and the template is Jesus Christ. Jesus is the perfect example of a Man who lived with *Purpose,* and as you wrap up this week on authentic identity, your own sense of purpose should begin to be revealed to you.

FAITH

For if we are faithful to the end, trusting God just as firmly as when we first believed, we will share in all that belongs to Christ (Hebrews 3:14 NLT).

This week we are addressing the characteristics of an authentic person having to do with the importance of identity. Last week, we talked about the characteristics of "focus" and "order"—focusing our thoughts by ordering our day. Some days this seems to come easier than others. It's not always easy to master your time and your mind in the most effective manner. This is where faith comes in.

Believing faith will keep you rooted and grounded in authenticity. It is by faith you preserve your soul. The writer of Hebrews wrote: *"We are of those who believe and by faith preserve the soul"* (Heb. 10:39 AMP). Take charge of your day, your thoughts—and your soul—by faith.

I've grown certain that the root of all fear is that we've been forced to deny who we are. —Frances Moore Lappe

ACTION STEPS

 Stir up your faith every moment of every day. Write down things that encourage your faith and place them where you can see them daily.

 Pinpoint those things you struggle with on a day-to-day basis that keep you from making the most of your time or distract you in the arena of your mind. How can you start removing these distractions?

 Exercise your faith—declare what you need and confess victory over the hindrances keeping your authentic self from shining through.

Through Him we received both the generous gift of His life and the urgent task of passing it on to others…. You are who you are through this gift and call of Jesus Christ! (Romans 1:5-6)

Day Twenty-two

GRATITUDE

Serve the Lord your God with joyfulness of [mind and] heart [in gratitude] for the abundance of all [with which He had blessed you] (Deuteronomy 28:47 AMP).

Your thought life is critical to the health of your soul. And there's nothing more critical to the health of your thought life than your attitude! You've heard it said that attitude determines altitude. Today, I want to propose that it's an attitude of gratitude that determines the degree to which you will be able to live true to your authentic self.

How grateful are you for who God created you to be? Gratitude for your unique combination of strengths, abilities, and special gifts will enable you to stay true to your calling.

Look for opportunities to be grateful and to show gratitude!

"Stay alert, with your eyes wide open in gratitude" (Col. 4:2).

Just as you can never "out-bless" God, you can never thank Him enough either.

The unthankful heart discovers no mercies; but let the thankful heart sweep through the day and, as the magnet finds the iron, so it will find, in every hour, some heavenly blessings! —Henry Ward Beecher

ACTION STEPS

- What five strengths, abilities, or talents about yourself are you grateful for?

- List five opportunities or outcomes that you have not yet experienced that you can preemptively be grateful for (now you are building faith!).

- Who are the people in your life you are especially grateful for? What can you do to make this known to them—and when?

- How much time do you invest praising and thanking God, focusing on all the good gifts and blessings He has bestowed—versus the time you spend focusing on all that is wrong and not what you imagine it should be?

I thank Christ Jesus our Lord, who has given me strength to do His work. He considered me trustworthy and appointed me to serve Him (1 Timothy 1:12 NLT).

DESTINY

I'll show up and take care of you as I promised and bring you back home. I know what I'm doing. I have it all planned out—plans to take care of you, not abandon you, plans to give you the future you hope for (Jeremiah 29:11).

Today I want to talk about destiny as it relates to living authentically. Your divine self has a divine destiny! Over and over in the Bible we read how God orchestrates our destinies—how He has called and anointed all who would *"only believe"* (Mark 5:36) to step forward and *"be strong and courageous"* (Josh. 1:6) in taking possession of all He has prepared for them.

To live true to your authentic self, you must continually choose to focus on your prospective future as opposed to your current position. Your present self is but the bud of the full flower you are destined to become—but it's up to you to decide whether or not you will bloom.

Your destiny is decision oriented. If you do not like where you are, make a decision to be somewhere else. You are always only one decision away from living the life of your dreams.

Destiny is no matter of chance. It is a matter of choice. It is not a thing to be waited for; it is a thing to be achieved. —William Jennings Bryan

ACTION STEPS

🦶 What do you hear God saying about who He has called you to be?

🦶 Paint a picture in your mind of your greatest possible future—write down what you see.

You guide me with Your counsel, leading me to a glorious destiny (Psalm 73:24 NLT).

Day Twenty-four

IDENTITY

In a word, what I'm saying is, "Grow up." You're kingdom subjects. Now live like it. Live out your God-created identity. Live generously and graciously toward others, the way God lives toward you (Matthew 5:48).

As you journey toward authenticity, you must have a strong sense of identity—you must know who you are! Being confident in who God has called you to be is vital to the health of your soul and essential to your empowerment. Peter wrote, *"Once you had no identity as a people; now you are God's people"* (1 Pet. 2:10 NLT).

You carry the DNA of your Heavenly Father. Your authentic, divine self is the seed of greatness God put on the inside of you—the deposit God made when He formed *"Christ in you, the hope of glory"* (Col. 1:27 NKJV). Embrace the glory within you. God hid the potential for greatness, success, and prosperity within your identity code. Much like our genetic code, your identity code is established at the moment of conception. It provides the schematics of how you were designed to function. Crack your identity code and the contours of your life will shift and your capacity to do great things will increase.

Only by constant and continual renewal of your spirit, soul, and mind will you be able to change your beliefs about the capacity you carry for greatness. "Live out your God-created identity!"

Your identity and your success go hand in hand. Many people sacrifice their identities by not doing what they really want to do. And that's why they're not successful. —Lila Swell

ACTION STEPS

🦶 What does "greatness" look like to you?

🦶 If you were truly living as a king and priest, or even simply as a "new creation in Christ," how would that look? How would it feel? How would you be different?

🦶 Get a vision for your God-created identity and write down everything you see.

Those who worship Him must do it out of their very being, their spirits, their true selves (John 4:24).

PURPOSE

Before I formed you in the womb I knew [and] approved of you [as My chosen instrument], and before you were born I separated and set you apart, consecrating you (Jeremiah 1:5 AMP).

An understanding of purpose is essential for authentic living, not only understanding your divine purpose overall, but also living purposefully—or being purpose-minded. In other words, there is living true to your calling and assignment in a general sense, but there is also being purposeful in regards to everything you do. It is a mindset as much as it is a discipline.

God created you on purpose for a purpose. It is up to you to be purposeful in understanding and firmly grasping what that purpose is. You must be intentional, deliberate, circumspect, and mindful.

It is up to you to press in to hear what God has purposed for you—and then to obey what you hear. Jesus said, *"If you refuse to do your part, you cut yourself off from God's part"* (Matt. 6:15).

The soul which has no fixed purpose in life is lost; to be everywhere, is to be nowhere. —Michel Eyquem De Montaigne

ACTION STEPS

🐾 Take time today to reflect on God's purposes and how those are reflected in your own. How intentionally are you pursuing this on a daily basis?

🐾 Write down what you hear God saying about His purpose for you in the season you are in now. Pay close attention to what God's Spirit is speaking to yours. Remember, the closer you listen, the more understanding you will be given.

🐾 What can you be doing more of to "do your part" in bringing God's purpose for your life to pass? What should you be doing less of? Heed this advice from Proverbs: *"Form your purpose by asking for counsel, then carry it out using all the help you can get"* (Prov. 20:18).

May He grant you according to your heart's desire, and fulfill all your purpose (Psalm 20:4 NKJV).

THE POWER OF WORDS

Pray! Ask The Word Incarnate to enlighten you regarding the power of words.

REVIEW YOUR STEPS (15 MINS)

Review the fifth week. Encourage members to share observations, comments, or ask questions.

VIDEO/TEACHING (30 MINS)

DRILLING DOWN (30 MINS)

- God's Word carries immense creative power and always accomplishes what He intends it to! Read Isaiah 55:10-11 aloud.

- Words are powerful, and can be dangerous! Life and death are in the power of the tongue. Read Proverbs 18:21. How have you experienced this truth—either on the life side of it, or the death side?

- Where are you heading, and what will it look like when you get there? Spend time this week pondering this… let your imaginations take over! Read, write, study, paint or draw what it would look like. Then line up your words and *talk* about it!

- When we read the Bible, we need to take God's Word personally. His promises are for His people, and if you have received Him as your Lord and Savior, that means you! Make God's Word personal by inserting your name in the promises He gives. What does this mean to you? How much more 'real' does this make His promises?

- What must happen in your heart for there to be a change in your mouth? How can you 'speak for a change'?

JOURNEY PLANS FOR THE NEXT WEEK

Point out Day 26–Day 30 in the book and journal. Encourage everyone to participate fully in this journey in order to get the most out of it.

CLOSE IN PRAYER

Week Six
Video Listening Guide

Words can drop like acid and create holes in our souls.

Your <u>brain</u> and your <u>flesh</u> don't want to go on a spiritual journey!

> *For the word of God is quick, and powerful, and sharper than any two-edged sword, piercing even to the dividing asunder of soul and spirit, and of the joints and marrow, and is a discerner of the thoughts and intents of the heart* (Hebrews 4:12 KJV).

<u>Favor</u> is attached to right living, living authentically.

<u>Grace</u> is attached to wrong living, covering the things that are inauthentic.

<u>Integrity</u> refers to being single and whole.

The more authentic you become, the more freedom you give to other people to be authentic.

There are things you pray aside, and others you lay aside.

What do you want?

The last place of your healing is where you're living emotionally right now.

Words are images clothed in a language.

The Soul Fast is trying to get to the root of the problem, and heal it. Then we don't have the fruit that affects our behavior.

Why am I doing the things that I'm doing?

*If you only deal with the **what**, the **why** is going to stay there, and the **what** will stay there too.*

THE POWER OF WORDS: HEALING THE HOLE IN YOUR SOUL

God created words as containers to fill with our faith. Your words frame your world with great power and authority if you work in union with God. Learning to live authentically is about learning to speak truthfully about who you really are—it's about living congruently so that what you say and do align with your core values and divine nature. It's about being formed and molded—mind and mouth—into the divine blessing God created you to become. The topics that relate to this week's theme are *Eating, Legislating, Asking, Sowing,* and *Blessing.*

Eating refers to consuming the words of God—His Holy Scriptures. The characteristic related to this is *Integrity*—being true to your genuine essence as a unique reflection of God's glory, which happens when you have taken His words inside yourself.

Legislating is when you use your words to direct others and bring about God's will on Earth. This role carries a great deal of *Responsibility.*

Asking is how you use your words to recognize that you don't know everything and you need God's direction. When you ask, He will reveal to you areas of *Potential* that you didn't even realize existed!

Our words can plant seeds of truth in others and in ourselves—this is the power of *Sowing.* When we sow those seeds of truth in our own thinking, they will sprout into the characteristic of *Impeccability*—speaking and living the truth we have sown.

The highest use of your words is *Blessing*—setting your words free on God's behalf. The characteristic that often moves you to bless is *Compassion,* which is love in action. And love in action causes you to bless!

INTEGRITY

*He trained us first, passed us like silver through refining fires, brought
us into hardscrabble country, pushed us to our very limit, road-tested
us inside and out...finally He brought us to this well-watered place*
(Psalm 66:10-12).

Learning to live authentically is all about learning to be true to who you really are—
it's about living congruently so that what you say and do align with your core values and
divine nature. It's about being formed and molded into the divine blessing God created
you to be.

Living with integrity is more than "moral rectitude"—it is also being true to your
genuine essence as a unique reflection of God's glory. When you are under pressure, what
is revealed? Do you remain strong and immoveable when it comes to who God has called
you to be?

Have you remained true to your purpose—to your passions? Have you been distracted
or derailed by circumstances—or have you continued to actively pursue those things that
make you feel most alive?

Try not to become a man of success but rather try to become a man of value.
—Albert Einstein

ACTION STEPS

🦶 What are the circumstances in your life making you stronger? What is tempering you and testing your integrity?

🦶 Clarity of intent, purity of motives, honest decision-making, congruency, and transparency are all included within the concept of *integrity*. Pray and ask God to assist you in securing these virtues in your life.

🦶 As a result of this refining process, write down what you know in your heart will be revealed. What treasure are you carrying inside of you that needs to find expression in the world around you?

Teach believers with your life: by word, by demeanor, by love, by faith, by integrity (1 Timothy 4:12).

RESPONSIBILITY

They heard the alarm but ignored it, so the responsibility is theirs. If they had listened…they could have saved their lives (Ezekiel 33:5 NLT).

Over the course of the past five weeks, we have talked a great deal about your power—and essentially your obligation—to choose and decide for yourself whether or not you will live authentically and true to your divine nature. Do you realize the responsibility you have to the world to become who God is calling you to be?

It is up to you to guard your heart, govern your mindset, harness your thoughts, discipline your behavior, and direct your words. *You* must take responsibility.

I pray you will be among those who hear, *"Well done, good and faithful servant!"* (Matt. 25:21 NIV). Remember, no one else can take responsibility for your life, your purpose, or your destiny other than you.

> Accept responsibility for your life. Know that it is you who will get you where you want to go, no one else. —Les Brown

ACTION STEPS

🐾 What are the abilities God has given you? How well are you stewarding them?

🐾 Has God called you to be a leader? Of course He has! The question is: How are you taking responsibility for fulfilling that call?

🐾 What one thing can you change that will change everything?

I want to remind us all that the world is listening, all the time. How we are ripples out from us into the world and affects others. We have a responsibility—an ability to respond—to the world. Finding our particular way of living this responsibility, of offering who we are to the world, is why we are here. We are called because the world needs us to embody the meaning in our lives. God needs us awake. The world we live in is a co-creation, a manifestation of individual consciousness woven into a collective dream. How we are with each other as individuals, as groups, as nations and tribes, is what shapes that dream. —Oriah Mountain Dreamer

A faithful, sensible servant is one to whom the master can give the responsibility of managing... (Luke 12:42 NLT).

POTENTIAL

None of these things move me, neither count I my life dear unto myself,
so that I might finish my course with joy, and the ministry, which I
have received of the Lord Jesus (Acts 20:24 KJV).

As we journey toward authenticity, we are striving to peel away the falsehoods, façades, and other fetters that keep us from maximizing our true potential.

Potential is unused and unrealized power to do and to become. And that's what this Soul Fast is all about—building your capacity for the great things God has in store for you. Refuse to be among those who never explore the hidden potential that lies deep within— refuse to sit in front of the television being entertained by other people's success. When you muster up the courage to leave the shoreline of comfort and familiarity, you can become all that you are destined to be.

Yes, you have the potential to do all sorts of things, but you need to focus on the thing God has assigned you alone to do. Understand what your assigned "craft" is—and then master it and sail it!

> Man's main task in life is to give birth to himself, to become what he poten-
> tially is. The most important product of his effort is his own personality.
> —Erich Fromm

ACTION STEPS

🐾 What is keeping you from total expression of all that you were meant to be, to do, and to accomplish? What are the weights, doubts, fears, and other encumbrances keeping you from fully expressing your divine self?

🐾 Ask God, "What is my assignment?"

🐾 Ask yourself, "What have I invested in maximizing my potential in that area?"

🐾 Envision what your potential maximized would look like. Now, imagine how it might look with God working in and through you! Ask God to show you, and then ask Him to do it!

No eye has seen, no ear has heard, and no mind has imagined what God has prepared for those who love Him (1 Corinthians 2:9 NLT).

IMPECCABILITY

Don't say anything you don't mean…You only make things worse when you lay down a smoke screen of pious talk, saying, "I'll pray for you," and never doing it, or saying, "God be with you," and not meaning it. You don't make your words true by embellishing them with religious lace. In making your speech sound more religious, it becomes less true. Just say "yes" and "no." When you manipulate words to get your own way, you go wrong (Matthew 5:33-37).

Impeccability. I love this word. I love this characteristic. Impeccability is what kept satan from having any power over Jesus (see John 14:30 NLT). Where sin leads to defeat and death, impeccability leads to victory and increasingly abundant life.

So how do we adopt this characteristic into our everyday lives? I think of John 1:47 where Jesus said of Nathanael,

"Here is an Israelite indeed…in whom there is no guile" (John 1:47 AMP). Or, as other translations say, *"no deceit"* (NKJV), *"nothing false"* (NCV), and *"a man of complete integrity"* (NLT). In other words, a man who is honest, transparent, has nothing to hide, who is living life inside out, a man who is living authentically, *"free of error, mixed motives, or hidden agendas"* (1 Thess. 2:3).

Authenticity has to do with honesty—do you always speak the truth? Do you say one thing when you mean another or misrepresent what you are truly feeling or thinking? The Bible speaks of one thing alone that makes a person perfect, and that is perfectly true words. James wrote, *"If anyone does not stumble in word, he is a perfect man"* (James 3:2 NKJV).

Be impeccable with your word. Speak with integrity. Say only what you mean. Avoid using the word to speak against yourself or to gossip about others. Use the power of your word in the direction of truth and love. —Miguel Angel Ruiz

ACTION STEPS

🦶 Do you always speak the truth? Do you say one thing when you mean another or misrepresent what you are truly feeling or thinking?

🦶 How have you used words against yourself?

🦶 How "free of error, mixed motives, or hidden agendas" are you living? How transparent is your life and speech?

🦶 Would Jesus say of you, "Look, there goes a person in whom there is no guile"?

If you could find someone whose speech was perfectly true, you'd have a perfect person, in perfect control of life (James 3:2 MSG).

COMPASSION

It's quite simple…be compassionate and loyal in your love, and don't take yourself too seriously (Micah 6:8).

In the last few days, we've talked about *responsibility, potential,* and *impeccability.* Today, I want to talk to you about *compassion*—because without this characteristic, you will have a difficult time fully walking in any of the other characteristics of an authentic person. American author, Frederick Buechner said, "Compassion is sometimes the fatal capacity for feeling what it is like to live inside somebody else's skin. It is the knowledge that there can never really be any peace and joy for me until there is peace and joy finally for you too."

I encourage you today to check your compassion meter. Open your heart and mind to those in need around you and explore how you might respond to those needs. Speak a blessing into the lives of everyone you encounter.

What better way is there to share the love of God than to bless others with your words? That is how you shine light into dark places!

> Too often we underestimate the power of a touch, a smile, a kind word, a listening ear, an honest accomplishment, or the smallest act of caring, all of which have the potential to turn a life around. —Leo Buscaglia

ACTION STEPS

🦶 Think of someone you normally don't have patience for, and speak a blessing over him or her now.

🦶 The next time you come across a person less fortunate, stop and bless them with your words. You might not have the money or time to invest, but you always have a kind word—and there is no better investment than that.

So be merciful (sympathetic, tender, responsive, and compassionate) even as your Father is (Luke 6:36 AMP).

THE POWER OF DOING

Pray! Ask the Holy Spirit to show you His heart about the power of doing.

REVIEW YOUR STEPS (15 MINS)

Review the sixth week. Encourage members to share observations, comments, or ask questions.

VIDEO/TEACHING (30 MINS)

DRILLING DOWN (30 MINS)

The purpose of fasting in the life of the believer is to take "self" off the throne and allow God's love to reign there instead.

❧ Read Isaiah 58:6-10 aloud.

❧ Think about and discuss God's chosen fast in light of 1 Cor. 13:1-13.

❧ In other words, if we don't walk in the fruit of the Spirit, then the gifts of the Spirit are useless. What is the fruit in your life from having removed the junk in your heart, the clutter from your mind, and the entanglements from your soul?

❧ What is different about you as a result of this 40-day Soul Fast?

❧ Encourage your members to pray about sharing their testimony of changes throughout this Soul Fast at the final meeting.

JOURNEY PLANS FOR THE NEXT WEEK

Point out Day 31–Day 35 in the book and guide. Encourage everyone to participate fully in this journey in order to get the most out of it.

CLOSE IN PRAYER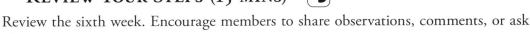

Week Seven
Video Listening Guide

You cannot give God what you don't have. You've got to get in the driver's seat first, before you can be free to choose to hand control over to Him.

If we resent <u>people</u>, we will also resent <u>God</u>.

We run to people who don't know who they are and ask them to tell us who we are.

You will always <u>resemble</u> those with whom you <u>assemble</u>.

The enemy doesn't <u>fight</u> what he doesn't <u>fear</u>.

What about you is the enemy fighting?

*There are things that you can **pray** aside, and there are things you must **lay** aside.*

I don't have to be afraid of life and afraid of the enemy, because the enemy is afraid of me.

"The greatest gift you can give yourself is the gift of change."

What if you have prayed and prayed for your family, community, government, and you are the answer?

The Power of Doing: God's Chosen Fast

The debate over whether people should focus on who they are or what they do is as ancient as the Torah itself. God created both, and they cannot be easily separated. In a previous week you looked at who you are regarding your identity apart from what you do—this week you will focus on the *do* part of you. The focus topics of *doing* are *Helping, Partnering, Continuing, Prioritizing*, and *Willing*.

Helping will require you to believe the best of people. Believing in people will lead you into this day's characteristic—showing *Respect* for others.

Your chances of thriving in life are considerably higher if you are *Partnering* with someone else who is also thriving. When you have locked arms with such quality people, make sure to place a high value on *Loyalty*—keep them around!

As you are *Continuing* through this Soul Fast, you are always one decision away from changing the course of your life and from living the life of your dreams. Your choices and behaviors establish your *Credibility*.

The highest priority on your list must always be staying connected to the Presence of God and listening to His still, small voice. *Prioritizing* God—things above selfish desires will help you live a life characterized by *Temperance*.

Finally, be *Willing* to run headlong into your destiny. Learning to harness the power of holiness by doing things God's way—by developing strong *Morality*—will bring you true success and freedom.

Day Thirty-one

RESPECT

Make the Master proud of you by being good citizens. Respect the authorities, whatever their level; they are God's emissaries for keeping order. It is God's will that by doing good, you might cure the ignorance of the fools who think you're a danger to society. Exercise your freedom by serving God, not by breaking the rules. Treat everyone you meet with dignity. Love your spiritual family. Revere God. Respect the government (1 Peter 2:13-17).

Akin to showing compassion is showing respect. Without the ability to respect the rights, opinions, and differences of others, you won't be able to show compassion toward those who might not think or look or behave like you.

If you want to be respected, you must show respect. This is why humility comes before honor. Those who are unable to honor and respect all people will themselves never become honorable.

The Bible tells us to *"show respect for all people"* (1 Pet. 2:17 NCV) and *"show respect and honor to them all"* (Rom. 13:7 NCV). You cannot "demand" respect, but only "command" it by taking action on behalf of others.

There is no better way to thank God for your sight than by giving a *helping* hand to someone in the dark. —Helen Keller

Do what you can, with what you have, where you are. —Theodore Roosevelt

ACTION STEPS

🦶 What one thing can you do today to honor someone?

🦶 To what degree do you command respect? Are you a leader others look up to because you are respectful—as in "full of respect?"

He rekindles burned-out lives with fresh hope, restoring dignity and respect to their lives—a place in the sun (1 Samuel 2:6).

LOYALTY

Don't lose your grip on Love and Loyalty. Tie them around your neck; carve their initials on your heart. Earn a reputation for living well in God's eyes and the eyes of the people (Proverbs 3:3-4).

Last week we focused on the power of our words, highlighting the authentic characteristics of impeccability, compassion, and respect—demonstrating that our words are simply a reflection of what is in our hearts. Beyond words is how we choose to behave—what we choose to do and the decisions we make every moment of every day.

If you want to lock arms and do life with quality people of understanding who are trustworthy and loyal, you will have to prove yourself loyal.

The degree to which you show yourself loyal to God—faithful, obedient, being true to your word, making good on your obligations and promises, and God-fearing—will determine to what extent you are able to live authentically.

Loyalty is the pledge of truth to oneself and others. —Ada Velez-Boardley

ACTION STEPS

🦶 How is God's loyalty working in *and* through your life?

🦶 In what areas might your loyalties be "divided"? What can you do to change that?

🦶 How has someone's disloyalty affected you in the past? Sometimes reflecting on that will compel you be more loyal.

Do not waver, for a person with divided loyalty is as unsettled as a wave of the sea that is blown and tossed by the wind…. Their loyalty is divided between God and the world, and they are unstable in everything they do (James 1:6, 8 NLT).

CREDIBILITY

Remove impurities from the silver and the silversmith can craft a fine chalice; remove the wicked from leadership and authority will be credible and God-honoring (Proverbs 25:4-5).

This week we are focusing on the power of doing. What we do is a result of the decisions we make and the actions we take as a result. You are always one decision away from changing the course of your life and from living the life of your dreams. Your choices and behaviors establish your credibility.

Credibility simply means "believability." Are you someone who says one thing and does another? Can people believe what you say? Without establishing your credibility—your believability—you will never be true to yourself. There is no deception worse than self-deception! You must hold yourself accountable for your own legitimacy, genuineness, and yes, authenticity. This is what lasting reputations are built upon.

> Ultimately, *you* are the product. *You* are the dream, the service, the idea, the message, even the Gospel made flesh.

> The more you are willing to accept responsibility for your actions, the more credibility you will have. —Brian Koslow

ACTION STEPS

🦶 Consciously strive to create credibility. Practice proven credibility boosters such as being honest, being on time, being a person of your word—being dependable.

🦶 What is your promise to the world? Establishing credibility is only a means to an end, not the end itself. What can people count on you to do because you are here? What do you stand for? How will you leave your mark?

He honoureth those who fear the Lord, those who revere the Lord. He who sweareth an oath, or who promiseth, to his neighbour, and deceiveth him not (Psalm 15:4 WYC).

TEMPERANCE

Yes, in the past you lived the way the world lives, following the ruler of the evil powers that are above the earth. That same spirit is now working in those who refuse to obey God. In the past all of us lived like them, trying to please our sinful selves and doing all the things our bodies and minds wanted (Ephesians 2:2-3 NCV).

You don't hear much about the characteristic of "temperance" these days. Temperance is sort of an old-fashioned word that is defined as "moderation in action, thought, or feeling: restraint—habitual moderation in the indulgence of the appetites or passions."

We have actually spoken a great deal about taming the appetites as a central purpose for this 40-Day Soul Fast—making *"no provision for [indulging] the flesh"* (Rom. 13:14 AMP) and abstaining *"from fleshly lusts, which war against the soul"* (1 Pet. 2:11 KJV).

Temperance is one of the seven attributes we are told to *"add to our faith"* by Peter (see 2 Peter 1:5-7) and one of the nine fruits of the Spirit Paul wrote to the Galatians about. (See Gal. 5:22-23.)

Great leaders have fallen because of their lack of self-control. Accomplished men and women of God have compromised their faith and ministry simply because they were unable to exercise restraint.

Don't use your lack of moderation or self-restraint in some area to keep you from your better self.

Being forced to work, and forced to do your best, will breed in you temperance and self-control, diligence and strength of will, cheerfulness and contentment, and a hundred virtues which the idle will never know. —Charles Kingsley

ACTION STEPS

☛ Examine your life. Where might the enemy have a foothold in the door of your soul, causing you to stumble in some area?

☛ What can you do to "clean house" in order to make sure you are *"temperate in all things?"* What might your little "excesses" say to others about you?

Moderation is better than muscle, self-control better than political power (Proverbs 16:32).

MORALITY

It is obvious what kind of life develops out of trying to get your own way all the time...a stinking accumulation of mental and emotional garbage; frenzied and joyless grabs for happiness...paranoid loneliness; cutthroat competition; all-consuming-yet-never-satisfied wants; a brutal temper; an impotence to love or be loved; divided homes and divided lives; small-minded and lopsided pursuits; the vicious habit of depersonalizing everyone into a rival; uncontrolled and uncontrollable addictions (Galatians 5:19-21).

This week we are talking about what I call "the power of doing." What you *do* can be as toxic to your soul as what you *think* or *say*—your actions have as much power to pollute or purify as your thoughts and words.

Morality simply means virtuous conduct—"behavior or qualities judged to be good"—based on a set of principles distinguishing between right and wrong or good and bad behavior. It's doing things God's way. It is drawing the line in the sand and saying this far and no further. Morality is a serious thing. Barry McGuire said, "And there was a real shedding of the old dogma, like boundaries of morality were being broken down and everybody was into the new party mode...which destroyed thousands of us."

In this success-driven society, it is odd to think that the bottom line might not be what we expect it is—success might not look like we think it does. At the end of the day, morality boils down to a life-and-death issue. We cannot afford to sit on the wall of indifference and expect society to change all by itself. As with beautiful art, the lines of morality must be deliberately drawn.

I never did, or countenanced, in public life, a single act inconsistent with the strictest good faith; having never believed there was one code of morality for a public, and another for a private man. —Thomas Jefferson

ACTION STEPS

🐾 Are you having difficulty "directing your energies wisely"? Check to make sure you're doing whatever you do "God's way" and not your own way.

🐾 Stop and reflect for a few moments on the verse above. Are any of the indicators listed here of "what happens when you do things your own way" present in your life?

We find ourselves involved in loyal commitments, not needing to force our way in life, able to marshal and direct our energies wisely" (Galatians 5:22-23).

SEALING THE HEALING

Pray! Ask the Risen Lord to give you new ways to celebrate His life-changing Spirit in you.

REVIEW YOUR STEPS (15 MINS)

Review the seventh week. Encourage members to share observations, comments, or ask questions.

VIDEO/TEACHING (30 MINS)

DRILLING DOWN (30 MINS)

Feast days and celebrations have always been significant in the life of God's people. Israel was commanded, and we as believers are still commanded, to stop and celebrate—or commemorate—and give glory to the One who brings the blessing and makes all things new. Why is this a command?

God understood the necessity for His people to establish regular intervals to stop and reconnect, to recall their true identity in relation to their Heavenly Father and the Creator of all things. What does this reconnection do for us?

Seal the healing of your soul by giving thanks and glorifying God for all He has done!

JOURNEY PLANS FOR THE NEXT WEEK

Next week is the last meeting you will have with this group. Remind members that you would love to have them share their testimony at the next meeting. If you will be having a "celebration," make sure to plan refreshments, etc.

Encourage the new leaders that you have identified to consider planning to lead a group of their own. Offer to assist them if you are able. Encourage them to pass the healing forward—until we have healed the world by healing our own soul!

CLOSE IN PRAYER

Week Eight
Video Listening Guide

Now abide faith, hope, love, these three; but the greatest of these is love (1 Cor. 13:13 NKJV)

Spiritual warfare does not <u>disappear</u> when we start to live authentically.

The more authentic you become, the more humble you will become.

Tolerance is giving people permission to be <u>different</u>.

Reach out beyond yourself and demonstrate the healing power of love.

We can see the world healed through love.

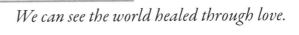

If there was one characteristic from this week that you would choose to "champion," which one would it be and why?

In one or two sentences, describe your experience over the last eight weeks.

Week Eight

Sealing the Healing: The Cleansing Power of Love

In this final week of *The 40 Day Soul Fast*, we are talking about the power of love at work in our lives. Truly authentic people reach a place where the love of God is activated in their lives and in their dealings with others. Love is the capstone on this eight-week journey—the greatest expression of the most authentic you.

As we look at the power of love, we address themes of *Dancing, Accepting, Standing, Uniting,* and *Telling.*

Dancing means living life together with God—doing His work as a partner with Him and loving people in your actions. The characteristic of *Justice* will emerge when you're living together with God this way.

Authentic people have come to a place of *Accepting* those who are commonly marginalized. It's another way you can live out God's love for them. The world understands this attribute by the name of *Tolerance*, which is more than just "putting up with" differences. It gives you the capacity to be merciful.

Being and doing come down to this—*Standing*. Taking your place, your God-given destiny, and refusing to be moved. The characteristic is *Ethics*, because ethics are your guidelines and an excellent place to root yourself.

Breaking down barriers between people and drawing us closer together—that's *Uniting*. Uniting is living in community—in love. The characteristic of *Interdependence* means something similar—we are not ourselves alone; we need each other to live authentic lives!

The final step is *Telling* others—sharing our testimony with the world. This brings us into a close-knit *Community* of people who do life together, share their stories, and live in harmony with God, each other, and their authentic selves!

Day Thirty-six

JUSTICE

For unto us a Child is born, unto us a Son is given; and the government will be upon His shoulder. And His name will be called Wonderful, Counselor, Mighty God, Everlasting Father, Prince of Peace. Of the increase of His government and peace there will be no end, upon the throne of David and over His kingdom, to order it and establish it with judgment and justice from that time forward, even forever. The zeal of the Lord of hosts will perform this (Isaiah 9:6-7 NKJV).

Yesterday we talked about the characteristic of morality and why it is so important in your journey toward authenticity. Justice, like morality, has to do with our actions and behaviors. Justice, however, takes us one step further in that it has more to do with how we treat other people than it does following a set of principles regarding how we conduct our personal lives. Justice is about what we do on behalf of others.

A person who has a sense of justice treats others with fairness, is respectful of the rights and needs of others, and is non-partial when it comes to showing kindness and mercy. This person will feel compelled to intercede on behalf of those less fortunate or speak up on behalf of someone who is being treated unfairly.

Without justice and love, peace will always be the great illusion. —Archbishop Helder Pessoa Camara

ACTION STEPS

🦶 How might you be neglecting the weightier matters of justice and mercy?

🦶 What can you begin doing today to "serve people" and make sure evil does not thrive unopposed?

The Lord has told you, human, what is good; He has told you what He wants from you: to do what is right to other people, love being kind to others, and live humbly, obeying your God (Micah 6:8 NCV).

Day Thirty-seven

TOLERANCE

Through His faithfulness, God displayed Jesus as the place of sacrifice where mercy is found by means of His blood. He did this to demonstrate His righteousness in passing over sins that happened before, during the time of God's patient tolerance. He also did this to demonstrate that He is righteous in the present time, and to treat the one who has faith in Jesus as righteous (Romans 3:25-26 CEB).

God is much bigger than your view of Him, and He will use all kinds of people—especially those on the margins—to broaden your understanding of that. Your task is to love and accept them where they are. Human beings will never be able to fully "map" out God, but it will take the experiences of each one to even get a small glimpse.

Tolerance is the ability to accept the differences of others. It enables you to show patience, compassion, and charity.

Tolerance can also be defined as "the power or capacity of an organism to tolerate unfavorable environmental conditions." Imagine what that kind of power could do for you.

When you exercise tolerance, you are exercising your faith in the power of God's goodness to soften hearts and His grace to overpower evil.

When you find peace within yourself, you become the kind of person who can live at peace with others. —Mildred Lisette Norman

ACTION STEPS

🦶 How would you rate your capacity to tolerate unfavorable conditions? What does this say about your own degree of personal empowerment?

🦶 How are you harnessing the power of tolerance to change the hearts and lives of those around you? In what small way might you show a little more tolerance?

He who is slow to anger has great understanding, but he who is hasty of spirit exposes and exalts his folly (Proverbs 14:29 AMP).

Ethics

When you're kind to others, you help yourself; when you're cruel to others, you hurt yourself. Bad work gets paid with a bad check; good work gets solid pay. Take your stand with God's loyal community and live, or chase after phantoms of evil and die. God can't stand deceivers, but oh how He relishes integrity (Proverbs 11:17-20).

As we wind down our *40-Day Soul Fast*, we are talking about the importance of "being" and "doing"—the impact our behaviors and actions have on the world around us—and how that in turn is reflected back to us in the way we experience life.

We began this journey toward authenticity talking about the inner life of the soul. As we have progressed through the 40 days, we have moved out from our own internal awareness of the life of our soul to an understanding of the power of our thoughts, our identity, and our words. This week, we are talking about how all of these elements affect how we relate to others.

Becoming more authentic, more genuine, more "real" requires a deeper sense of truthfulness, honesty, and honor. Our truest intentions are revealed. Our integrity is tested. Our credibility is established. This is what the concept of *ethics* represents: That which is motivated by pure, noble, and honorable intentions—an uprightness in choices, values, business dealings, and professional aspirations. Your sense of ethics will require you to take a stand.

Those whose hearts are upright before God will be required to stand up on behalf of those can't stand up for themselves—to stand up for the oppressed—to stand up against evil! Let your life make a statement by taking a stand.

The ultimate measure of a man is not where he stands in moments of comfort
and convenience, but where he stands at times of challenge and controversy.
—Martin Luther King Jr.

ACTION STEPS

🐾 In bringing something to your attention, could God be requiring you to take a stand?

🐾 Write down some thoughts about the quote: "You are only as powerful as that for which you stand."

🐾 "Unless we stand for something, we shall fall for anything." How do you see this truth working in your own life?

If you don't take your stand in faith, you won't have a leg to stand on (Isaiah 7:9).

Day Thirty-nine

INTERDEPENDENCE

You can easily enough see how this kind of thing works by looking no further than your own body. Your body has many parts—limbs, organs, cells—but no matter how many parts you can name, you're still one body. It's exactly the same with Christ. By means of His one Spirit, we all said good-bye to our partial and piecemeal lives. We each used to independently call our own shots, but then we entered into a large and integrated life in which He has the final say in everything (1 Corinthians 12:12).

Whether you love people by giving financially, by sharing your wisdom and knowledge, or by exercising your gifts and talents, your life is directly united to others and is interdependent on their reciprocating acts of love toward you. Mark Twain once said: "To get the full value of joy you must have someone to divide it with." Love others lavishly—because in truth, you are showering love on yourself!

Yesterday we talked about ethics and taking a stand on behalf of others—today we will focus on why this is so important. Interestingly, the more authentic we become, the more interdependent we will be. As the dividing walls and facades come down, we learn to trust in and rely on one another—we realize we need each other to complete one another.

I can never be what I ought to be until you are what you ought to be. This is the way our world is made. No individual or nation can stand out boasting of being independent. We are interdependent. —Martin Luther King, Jr.

ACTION STEPS

🦶 How deep is your sense of interdependence?

🦶 Where do you fit in to bring more completion to the Body of Christ?

🦶 What dividing walls are you still putting up to keep yourself independent? What can you do to start taking them down today, one brick at a time?

In the same way, we are many, but in Christ we are all one body. Each one is a part of that body, and each part belongs to all the other parts (Romans 12:5 NCV).

Day Forty

Community

Above all things have intense and unfailing love for one another, for love covers a multitude of sins [forgives and disregards the offenses of others] (1 Peter 4:8 AMP).

Connection, collaboration, communication, acceptance, compassion, respect, support, safety, shared values, inclusion, kindness, tolerance, understanding, and inspiration are a few words that come to mind when I think of community. Our communities need to be healed, and we can start by healing our own souls so that we can walk in authentic love.

As we bring our journey to a close, I want to talk to you about what I believe is the nearest and dearest thing to God's heart: Building authentic community.

Building community is not a political or economic process, but purely spiritual and relational. It is ultimately about corporate destiny—our destiny as a collaborative entity. It is about living and working together so that we can make this world a better place for everyone.

When you build community, there is no big "I" and little "you," but simply "we" and "us."

This is what living in community is all about. It's God's best will for His people. It's what floods the world with light and turns it upside right.

And as we let our own light shine, we unconsciously give other people permission to do the same. As we are liberated from our own fear, our presence automatically liberates others.—Marianne Williamson

ACTION STEPS

🦶 From this day forward, how will you shine a little brighter? Describe what that might look like and the affect it could have on the people you encounter.

🦶 Change begins one thought, one soul, one life at a time. What is the one thought you can adopt that could change everything? What will be the new story you tell as a result?

🦶 How can you start a conversation in your community—whether it is the workplace, church, neighborhood, or school—about living more authentically?

Your love for one another will prove to the world that you are My disciples (John 13:35 NLT).

We can't help but thank God for you, because your faith is flourishing and your love for one another is growing (2 Thessalonians 1:3 NLT).

CELEBRATION!

Pray! Ask our Heavenly Father to show you new ways to celebrate His life-changing Spirit in you.

**This week is a time to celebrate with your members who have made great strides towards living more authentic lives. You may want to plan a celebration with festive decorations, favorite foods, music, and sharing of testimonies.

REVIEW YOUR STEPS (15 MINS)

Review the eighth week. Encourage members to share observations, comments, or ask questions.

VIDEO (30 MINS)

DRILLING DOWN (30 MINS)

🐜 Allow time for personal testimonies; affirm the healing of each soul!

🐜 Celebrate!

JOURNEY PLANS

This is the last meeting you will have with this group. Encourage the new leaders that you have identified to begin planning to lead a group of their own. Offer to assist them if you are able. Encourage them to pass the healing forward—until we have really healed the world by healing our own soul!

CLOSE IN PRAYER

147

DR. TRIMM'S BLESSING

I have the courage and personal integrity to:

- Be myself

- Dream about a better life

- Wake up and live the life of my dreams

- Enjoy today and believe that tomorrow will be better than today

- Voice my opinions

- Pursue my goals

- Change my mind

- Break self-destructive activities, thoughts, and cycles of failure

- Set clear boundaries for myself and help others to respect them

- Change for the best

- Be my best

- Give my best

- Do my best

- Put my best foot forward

- Enjoy giving and receiving life

- Face and transform my fears with courage

- Seek and ask for support when I need it

- Spring free from the super-person trap

- Stop being all things to everyone

- Trust myself to know what is right for me

- Make my own decisions based on my perceptions of options

- Befriend myself

- Be kind to myself

- Be totally honest with myself

- Respect my vulnerabilities

- Heal old and current wounds

- Acquire new, good, and useful habits and eliminate the bad

- Complete unfinished business

- View my failures as life lessons

- Turn my losses into gain

- Realize that I have emotional and practical rights

- Honor my commitments

- Keep my promises

- Give myself credit for my accomplishments

- Love the little girl/boy in me

- Overcome my addictions and need for approval

- Grant myself permission to laugh out loud

- Live life out loud

- Play as hard as I can

- Dance like no one is watching

- Sing at the top of my voice

- Color outside of the lines

- Watch Mother Nature as she tucks the sun in for a good night's sleep and then turns the nightlights on for my enjoyment, security, and pleasure

- Witness the dawning of a new day as the sun rubs lingering sleepiness from its eyes

- Choose life over death

- Choose success over failure

- Live with an attitude of gratitude
- Quit being a trash receptacle and dumping bin
- Rid myself of toxic relationships
- Pursue and develop healthy and supportive relationships
- Renegotiate the terms of all relationships
- Nurture myself like I nurture others
- Take "me moments"
- Be alone without feeling lonely
- Demand that people give to me as much as I give them
- Manage my time
- Value the time that God has given me by using it wisely
- Demand others to value my time
- Be more objective about my feelings and subjective about my thoughts
- Detoxify all areas of my life
- Take an emotional enema when necessary
- Nurture others because I want to not because I have to
- Choose what is right for me
- Insist on being paid fairly for what I do
- Know when enough is enough
- Say "No" and mean it
- Put an end to toxic cycles
- Set limits and boundaries
- Say "Yes" only when I really mean it
- Have realistic expectations
- Take risks and accept change
- Live morally
- Conduct my affairs ethically

- Grow through change
- Grow through challenges
- Give others permissions to grow and be themselves
- Break glass ceilings
- Live beyond the limits
- Set new goals
- Savor the mystery of the Holy Spirit
- Pray and expect an exceptional and favorable outcome
- Meditate in order to un-clutter my mind
- Wave good-bye to guilt, self-doubt, rejection, and insecurity
- De-weed the flower bed of my thought life
- Treat myself with respect and teach others to do the same
- Fill my own cup first, and then refresh others from the overflow
- Demand excellence from others and myself
- Plan for the future but live in the present
- Value my insight, intelligence, and wisdom
- Know that I am loveable
- Celebrate the differences in others
- Make forgiveness a priority
- Accept myself just as I am now and forever
- Live within my means
- Manifest His divinity
- Breathe beyond innate fears by living in the realm of faith
- Embrace His Spirit, which is stronger and wiser than mine
- Prosper beyond my imagination
- Give more than I receive
- Give to those who can never return the favor

- Love unconditionally
- Live consciously

Therefore, I will:

- Give God the time He needs
- Give my mind the order and peace it needs
- Give my life the discipline it needs
- Give my spirit the freedom it needs
- Give my soul the love it needs
- Give my body the nourishment and exercise it needs
- Give my voice the platform it needs
- Take a stand for what I believe
- Give myself the love and attention I need
- Pursue my dreams and accomplish my goals
- Pursue my purpose and maximize my potential
- Stand on truth and take a stand for truth
- Positively impact my generation
- Positively influence a system and/or an institution
- Live, learn, love, serve, and then leave a legacy

I am on a collision course with destiny: I am at the Intersection of Truth; the Avenue of Opportunity; the Boulevard of Passion; and on a Street named Courage. All lights are green. I choose to proceed. Today, I crash and walk away with purpose, success, and nobility. Today and always: I alone accept and own full and total responsibility for being my genuine and true self. Therefore, I vow to live authentically, to grow and care for my best and nobler self that I may reflect the shimmer of God's glory and divinity. Today, I shall be blessed with all good things. My day shall be good. I will have good success. My joy, peace, prosperity, and success shall be as abundant as the stars at night. Friendship, favor, affluence, influence, health, happiness, support, beauty, and abundant living shall be my constant companion. I am unconditionally loved, celebrated, revered, appreciated, and honored beyond measure and human comprehension. I make a difference in this world. This is my contract with myself. And today, I give myself permission to push until I succeed.

THE 40 DAY SOUL FAST HANDBOOK

SUGGESTED GUIDELINES FOR DETOXIFYING SPIRIT, SOUL, AND BODY

By Dr. Cindy Trimm

In consultation with Dr. Paula Walker M.D.

A Personal Word from Dr. Cindy Trimm

If you are reading this, you are taking part in the *40 Day Soul Fast*. Please remember the purpose of the Soul Fast is to eliminate the toxins in your soul, not your body. However, because the body and soul are interconnected, what is good for one is good for the other! I encourage you to take this opportunity to cleanse and detox your body even as you dedicate yourself to cleansing and detoxifying your soul.

The Body of Christ is longing for detoxification on so many levels. That is demonstrated by the large number of people who have asked me for information about detoxifying their entire system as they pursue this *40 Day Soul Fast*. I pray it will be a useful tool to help you along your "life-cleansing" journey.

Remember, Jesus said, *"It is not what goes into the mouth of a man that makes him unclean…but what comes out of the mouth; this makes a man unclean…whatever comes out of the mouth comes from the heart, and this is what makes a man unclean"* (Matthew 15:11, 18 AMP).

If you choose to pursue a physical fast along with the Soul Fast, please don't become distracted or burdened by the demands of a restrictive fasting regimen. I would encourage you to prayerfully allow God to lead you into laying aside whatever is keeping you from thinking more clearly, having more energy, or pursuing Him more fully. I would suggest along with fasting unhealthy foods, you fast unhealthy thoughts—as you give up toxic eating habits, give up toxic behaviors. It is more destructive to your soul to engage in gossip or complaining than it is to eat gravy or cupcakes.

The primary aim of the *40 Day Soul Fast* is to *"lay aside every weight, and the sin which so easily ensnares us, and let us run with endurance the race that is set before us"* (Heb. 12:1 NKJV). The weights of negative thought habits and toxic verbal behaviors tie you down and keep you vulnerable to sin. The debris in your mind and the junk coming out of (not going into) your mouth are what keep you stagnated and going around in circles. These are the toxins that prevent you from running with endurance and fulfilling your divine purpose—and cause so many to abort their God-given dreams.

If exercising the discipline of fasting unhealthy foods will help you be more mindful of exercising the discipline of fasting unhealthy thoughts, then let the two work together synergistically to help you bring your spirit, soul, and body into alignment. It is for this reason I am making this guide available—to help you learn to cleanse and renew your body even as you cleanse and renew your mind! May you be *empowered for life* and *empowered to live beyond your limits!*

SCRIPTURE REFERENCES

When this vision came to me, I, Daniel, had been in mourning for three whole weeks. All that time I had eaten no rich food. No meat or wine crossed my lips, and I used no fragrant lotions until those three weeks had passed (Daniel 10:2-3 NLT).

This is the kind of fast day I'm after: to break the chains of injustice, get rid of exploitation in the workplace; free the oppressed; cancel debts. What I'm interested in seeing you do is: sharing your food with the hungry, inviting the homeless poor into your homes, putting clothes on the shivering ill-clad, being available to your own families.

Do this and the lights will turn on, and your lives will turn around at once. Your righteousness will pave your way. The God of glory will secure your passage. Then when you pray, God will answer. You'll call out for help and I'll say, "Here I am."

If you get rid of unfair practices, quit blaming victims, quit gossiping about other people's sins, if you are generous with the hungry and start giving yourselves to the down-and-out, your lives will begin to glow in the darkness, your shadowed lives will be bathed in sunlight. I will always show you where to go. I'll give you a full life in the emptiest of places—firm muscles, strong bones. You'll be like a well-watered garden, a gurgling spring that never runs dry. You'll use the old rubble of past lives to build anew, rebuild the foundations from out of your past. You'll be known as those who can fix anything, restore old ruins, rebuild and renovate, make the community livable again (Isaiah 58:6-12 MSG).

It's not what goes into your body that defiles you; you are defiled by what comes from your heart (Mark 7:15 NLT).

Can't you see that the food you put into your body cannot defile you? Food doesn't go into your heart, but only passes through the stomach and then goes into the sewer." (By saying this, he declared that every kind of food is acceptable in God's eyes.)

And then he added, "It is what comes from inside that defiles you. For from within, out of a person's heart, come evil thoughts, sexual immorality, theft, murder, adultery, greed, wickedness, deceit, lustful desires, envy, slander, pride, and foolishness. All these vile things come from within; they are what defile you" (Mark 7:18-23 NLT).

We work to feed our appetites. Meanwhile our souls go hungry (Ecclesiastes 6:7 MSG).

THE "FAST" WAY TO HEALING AND HEALTH

Some people wear out one set of teeth digging their way to the grave, only to buy a false set of teeth to complete the task of eating themselves to death. — Author Unknown

Fasting—traditionally seen as a spiritual activity—is increasingly being used as a method to improve physical, mental, and emotional health. It is an ever-increasing belief that fasting not only helps to relieve the body of toxins, but also stimulates and increases spiritual awareness and produces growth hormones, which postpones the aging process. The search for health goes on unceasingly, and fasting has helped many to achieve it.

Contrary to what our minds may tell us, the body can function for seven days without water and forty days without food. I am not asking you to go forty days without food, but I do encourage you to practice one of the fasting options offered below for the duration of the *40 Day Soul Fast*. I believe your soul will benefit from any cleansing taking place in your body—and vice versa! *"Beloved, I pray that you may prosper in all things and be in health, just as your soul prospers"* (3 John 1:2 NKJV).

The following information is intended to give you a variety of options you can pursue, some general guidelines to follow, an array of basic information to consider, and other helpful tools you can use to cleanse your life—body, soul, and spirit.

Cleanse and nourish your body by avoiding all toxic products and unwholesome foods and hydrating sufficiently—no less than eight glasses of water per day!

Cleanse and nourish your soul by avoiding all toxic media and unwholesome entertainment—hydrate your soul by drinking from the fountain of the Word daily!

Cleanse and nourish your spirit by avoiding toxic places and unwholesome people—hydrate your spirit by praising and worshiping God whenever possible.

Be good to yourself—your true, authentic self—your soul.

Read The Creed provided at the back of this booklet everyday for the next 40 days.

*For the next 40 days, set aside 40 minutes each day to invest in the life of your soul.

WEEKLY:

1. Read each week's article post available for download at www.soulfast.com.

2. Listen to each week's video lesson.

DAILY:

3. Set aside a designated time and place to read the daily entry in the book and respond to the action steps in the participant's guide.

4. Pray that the Lord will reveal to you the specific toxins cluttering your own soul.

5. Praise God for the answers, solutions, and guidance He has promised.

6. Recite The Creed at the start of each day.

DETOX YOUR WHOLE SELF

Any good health program should include a system for detoxifying—or cleansing—the body of toxins. Detoxing is the process of removing harmful toxins from the body—the whole body—including the heart and mind.

You haven't completely detoxed until you've detoxed in the following ways:

PSYCHOLOGICALLY

An individual's psychological state of being will be a determining factor in overall physical health. People who are constantly under stress from career, lifestyle, financial, or marital pressures need to take time out to give not only the body a rest, but also the mind. Create space for "down-time" to relieve the mind of anything that causes undue stress and meditate on positive things.

It has been found that psychological and emotional symptoms are directly associated with excess toxins in the body. Create a peaceful atmosphere for yourself while focusing on detoxifying your system. Here are some pointers:

- ❧ Be aware of internal dialogue.

- ❧ Refuse negativity.

- ❧ Think positive thoughts.

- ❧ Change the things you can.

- ❧ Accept the things you cannot change.

EMOTIONALLY

The heavy demands that we are all subject to in today's world may give rise to stress, anxiety, mood swings, depression, tension, poor memory, forgetfulness, irritability, negativity, mental exhaustion, etc. and may render us less objective and effective in handling the affairs of the day. As you detox your body, detox your thoughts:

- Create a peaceful environment—incorporate fresh flowers.

- Clear your home and work environment of unnecessary clutter.

- Give away whatever you haven't used or worn in the past year.

- Play uplifting music in lieu of turning on the television.

- Just play! Play with your pet, play games, play an instrument.

- Be creative. Be adventurous. Explore a new craft or hobby.

- Watch a life-affirming movie.

- Exercise every day (ride a bike, take a brisk walk outdoors).

- Focus on fresh air! Get outside whenever you can!

- Take steam baths/saunas twice weekly.

- Take a bath in Epsom salts or baking soda to draw out impurities.

- Drink a minimum of eight glasses of water each day.

- Take time to rest and reflect daily.

- Smile at others and laugh at yourself.

- Hug your loved ones.

- Give thanks.

A NOTE FROM DR. PAULA WALKER

After prayer and consideration of the various factors involved in regards to the unique circumstances of the many individuals participating in the cleansing program (such as their health status, medication regimens, high-demand work schedules, rigorous lifestyles, personal fasting history, and so on), here are my suggestions for undergoing a long-term cleansing-type fast.

I do not recommend total fasting from food and liquid, especially water. The body needs at least two quarts of water each day to sustain life. The body can only go a few days without water. That being said, total fasting would be unsafe.

For the purpose of a 40-day fast, I do not recommend limiting intake to water-only. While water-only fasting has therapeutic benefits in certain cases where there is inflammation in the body (such as in cases of Osteoarthritis, Lupus, Rheumatoid Arthritis, Fibromyalgia, etc.), in general, water-only fasts are not well tolerated for extended periods of time and the liver (the detoxifying organ of the body) is mostly unsupported during a water-only fast. Also, water-only fasts are often associated with an unpleasant weakness that is counterproductive for active individuals. Furthermore, water-only fasts may lead to low potassium levels. Low potassium can cause life-threatening cardiac arrhythmias or abnormal heart rhythms. For these reasons, I would suggest eliminating this type of fast as an option.

Some options I would suggest for a 40 day fasting period would be the following:

FOR THE EXPERIENCED FASTER: THE MASTER CLEANSER FAST

Only consume water and the Master Cleanser beverage (recipe provided below) throughout the entire 40-day process. If an individual is on medication, he or she *must* consult his or her physician and follow the medication recommendations put forth by his or her doctor. Physician consultation is necessary because some medications will preempt one's ability to fast while other medications can be safely taken during a fast.

FOR THE INTERMEDIATE FASTER: A PARTIAL FAST

This option can include a sunup to sundown alternative—the faster can eat from 6:00 A.M. to 6:00 P.M. and then do a water-only fast from 6:00 P.M. to 6:00 A.M. With this model, eating is done during the day when the faster is actively engaged in activities and can use the additional dietary fuel and burn the excess calories, but this option can also be implemented vice versa with fasting occurring from 6:00 A.M. to 6:00 P.M. with eating beginning after 6:00 P.M.

Or, otherwise on this partial fast, the individual may eat only fruits and vegetables (during a specified time window) and drink water only during the entire 40-day fast; organic fruits and vegetables should be used when possible. The fruits and vegetables that are consumed should be consumed from 8:00 A.M. to 12:00 noon only. The individual can eat any variety or version of fruits and vegetables. After 12:00 noon, the individual should abstain from all whole fruit and vegetable intake. During the remaining 20 hours of the day (12:00 P.M. to 8:00 A.M.), preferably only water should be consumed. The Master Cleanser beverage may also be consumed, if the faster desires a cleansing, healthful beverage as an alternative to water. During the 20 hour water-only fasting period of each day, if the faster experiences overwhelming cravings that are unsatisfied by water or the Master Cleanser beverage, he or she should go ahead and have a serving of fruit and/or vegetables at that time and as needed.

Again, if an individual is on medication, he or she should consult his or her physician and follow the medication recommendations put forth by his or her doctor. Physician consultation is necessary because some medications will preempt one's ability to fast while other medications can be safely taken during a fast.

During this partial fast, it is suggested that no other food items be consumed besides any variety or version of fresh fruits and vegetables. No other beverages, other than those stated, should be consumed. All sodas, fruit juices, sweet tea, lemonade, coffee, lattes, and other drinks are to be avoided.

FOR THE BEGINNER FASTER: THE DANIEL FAST

The individual would eat no meat, no sweets and no bread. Throughout the 40 days, the individual would eat any variety or version of fruits, vegetables, legumes (peas, beans, nuts, etc) and certain dietary fibers, such as brown rice, steel-cut oatmeal (without butter, sugar, or other condiments), and drink water only as desired throughout the day. Meal variation may include a vegetable/legume plate with several servings of vegetables constituting one meal (e.g. squash, green beans, cabbage, and black eye peas, etc.), salads, vegetable soups, whole fruits, grilled vegetables, bean soup, vegetable and bean casserole, etc.

If an individual is on medication, he or she should continue to take them, unless directed otherwise by a physician. Physician consultation is necessary because some medications will preempt one's ability to fast while other medications can be safely taken during a fast.

This fast is recommended for the beginning faster as well as for Type II Diabetics, who have received medical clearance from their doctors to participate in the fast. Type II Diabetics should consult their physician about possible adjustments to their blood-sugar lowering medication regimen during the fasting season to avoid episodes of hypoglycemia or low blood sugar.

FOR FASTERS OF ALL LEVELS: THE JUICE FAST

For this type of fast, the individual will need a juicer and a variety of fresh fruits and vegetables. Juice fasting is beneficial for the body. It supports the liver and the detoxification process. It's less strenuous and it doesn't produce any undesirable weakness or fatigue. No solid foods will be consumed on this fast, just the juice of fresh fruits and vegetables and water. Organic produce is preferable and should be used whenever possible. Again, juices should be freshly prepared. No commercial fruit or vegetable juices should be used during the fast such as V-8, Tropicana, Snapple, etc.

If an individual is on medications, he or she should consult his or her physician and follow the medication recommendations put forth by his or her doctor. Physician consultation is necessary because some medications will preempt one's ability to fast while other medications can be safely taken during a fast.

For fresh fruit and vegetable juice recipes, I recommend Dr. Don Colbert's book entitled, *Toxic Relief.* The book may be purchased at any book retailer.

All of the above fasts are easy on the digestive system and will give the gastrointestinal system a Sabbath from the work and energy of digesting food. Since energy will not be expended by digesting dense foods, more energy will be available for other activities. In essence, the faster will feel energized! More importantly, all of the above fasts represent a sacrifice of some kind so the fasting option choice is a personal one, based on health status and the divine guidance of the Holy Spirit. God will honor the sacrifice!

Lastly, as part of the guidelines, please be advised that if you have questions or concerns about anything related to your health, you must consult your physician prior to beginning any type of fast. Any individual who has health issues or concerns in general about his or her physical ability to fast should consult his or her physician before beginning the fast.

The above fasting options are offered solely as suggestions. Anyone who follows them does so voluntarily and is advised to consult their physician beforehand. Since each individual will react differently to each fasting option, each person must use his or her own judgment as to its use and continuation throughout the proposed 40-day period.

FASTING GUIDELINES

Prior to beginning any type of fast, each participant should consult with his or her doctor.

As wonderful of a tool as fasting is for health and cleansing and detoxification purposes, there are some individuals who have certain conditions where fasting is contraindicated or prohibited.

Please keep the following in mind if you are considering the pursuit of a fast:

- Do not fast if you are pregnant or nursing.

- Do not fast if you have a serious illness like cancer, AIDS, Anorexia Nervosa, Leukemia, severe anemia, or if you are emaciated or malnourished as the result of another illness.

- Do not fast if you are a Type I Diabetic or Insulin-Dependent Diabetic.

- All Type II Diabetics (and some Type II Diabetics on insulin) should especially inquire of his or her physician about the feasibility of fasting and about any possible adjustments to the insulin/blood sugar-lowering medication regimen during the fasting period since the blood sugars tend to be lower during a fast. If diabetics receive medical clearance to do the fast, they should continue home monitoring of blood sugars throughout the fast as directed by their physician. Note: Of the options listed, the Daniel Fast is the most suitable option for Type II Diabetics, who have received medical clearance.

❧ Do not fast if you are taking a diuretic (or "water pill"). Diuretics precipitate loss of water and electrolytes like potassium. Do not fast if you have liver or kidney disease; the liver is the detoxifying organ of the body and the kidneys aid in the elimination of waste via the urine. If either of these organs is impaired, it will be difficult to obtain the usual benefits from fasting, and you may exacerbate your medical condition.

❧ Do not fast if you have congestive heart failure or a diagnosed cardiac arrhythmia.

❧ Do not fast if you are on certain medications like prednisone, narcotics, antidepressants, or diuretics. You should refrain from fasting if you are taking any of these medications. However, there are other medications that can be safely taken during a fast. Please consult your health care provider when considering a fast to determine if fasting is right for you.

Medications should not be discontinued abruptly. If a fasting participant is on medicine, he or she should consult his or her physician regarding possible adjustments to the medication regimen during the fasting regimen.

If the participant develops exacerbation of an existing medical illness or begins to develop adverse reactions or worrisome symptoms of any kind, he or she should discontinue the fast immediately and consult his or her physician immediately.

Distilled water is used for the Master Cleanser recipe; otherwise, if the faster is consuming water for hydration purposes with the other fasting options, spring or filtered water may be consumed.

Organic produce should be used whenever possible where fruits and vegetables are listed in the fasting options.

Fasters should be compassionate and gentle with themselves. During the fast, if they fall off the wagon and consume a restricted food or dietary item, they should acknowledge the detour (and enjoy it) and get back on the fast as soon as possible.

How you end a fast is just as important as how you start and conduct one. A typical post-fasting regimen for breaking a fast would look like the following, starting with the first day after the fast:

Day 1: Eat fresh fruit, especially fruits with the highest water content because these are the easiest to digest and assimilate. Note: On Day 1, avoid tropical fruits, such as pineapples and papayas, since these contain strong enzymes that might upset your stomach.

Day 2: You may have a combination of fresh fruits and vegetables throughout the day. For instance, you might choose to have fresh fruit for breakfast followed by vegetable soup for lunch and dinner.

Day 3: You will follow a similar diet as outlined for Day 2.

Day 4: You may add to the various fruits and vegetable soups a salad and/or a baked potato.

Day 5: Building on the diet from the previous four days, you may now introduce a small serving of lean (preferably organic) meat, such as chicken, turkey, or fish.

MASTER CLEANSER RECIPE*

The most convenient way to make the Master Cleanser beverage is by the gallon—that way it will last throughout the day.

You will need:

- ✤ The juice of 10 fresh organic lemons

- ✤ 1/8 tsp to 1/4 tsp of cayenne pepper

- ✤ 1 1/3 cup of grade B maple syrup

- ✤ 1 gallon of distilled, purified, or spring water [distilled water tends to yield a deeper cleanse and is often preferred for this reason]

Take the gallon of water and remove two cups of the water and place it aside in a separate, clean pitcher. To the remaining water in the gallon of distilled/spring water add the lemon juice, grade B maple syrup, and cayenne pepper. Afterwards, reintroduce the two cups of water to the gallon of distilled/spring water until the gallon bottle is full; lastly shake the gallon bottle to thoroughly mix the contents. The Master Cleanser beverage is now ready to be consumed. Additional grade B maple syrup may be added to taste. Refrigerate the unused portion of the Master Cleanser beverage to maintain its freshness.

One may drink as much of the Master Cleanser beverage as desired.

Here is the recipe for one 16 oz. glass or mug (may be consumed cold or hot):

2 TBSP fresh lemon juice (approx. 1/2 lemon)

2 TBSP genuine grade B maple syrup

1/10 tsp cayenne pepper (red pepper)

10-16 oz distilled, spring, or purified water

Combine the lemon juice, maple syrup, and cayenne pepper in a large glass or mug and fill with cold or hot water.

HOW TO BREAK THE MASTER CLEANSER FAST

Day 1 and Day 2: Drink several 8 oz. glasses of fresh orange juice as desired throughout the day. The orange juice prepares the digestive system to properly digest and assimilate regular food. Drink it slowly. If there has been any digestive difficulty prior to or during the changeover, extra water may be taken with the orange juice.

Day 3: Orange juice in the morning. Raw fruit should be consumed for lunch. Fruit or vegetable salad at night. You are now ready to eat normally.

(See Burroughs, Stanley. *The Master Cleanser*, Reno, NV: Burroughs Books, 1976.)

POWERFUL JUICE COMBINATIONS

By Paul C. Bragg

1. Beet, celery, and alfalfa sprouts

2. Cabbage, celery, and apple

3. Cabbage, cucumber, celery, tomato, spinach, and basil

4. Tomato, carrot, and mint

5. Carrot, celery, watercress, garlic, and wheatgrass

6. Grapefruit, orange, and lemon

7. Beet, parsley, celery, carrot, mustard greens, and garlic

8. Beet, celery, dulse, and carrot

9. Cucumber, carrot, and mint

10. Carrot, celery, parsley, onion, cabbage, and sweet basil

11. Carrot and coconut milk

12. Carrot, broccoli, lemon, and cayenne

13. Carrot, cauliflower, and rosemary

14. Apple, carrot, radish, and ginger

15. Apple, pineapple, and mint

16. Apple, papaya, and grapes

17. Papaya, cranberries, and apple

18. Grape, cherry, and apple

19. Watermelon (include seeds)

20. Leafy greens, broccoli, and apple

21. Beets, celery, and carrots

22. Asparagus, carrot, and mint

23. Watercress, cucumber, and garlic

24. Mission figs and water

25. Your own favorite combinations

Note: During your juice fast, in addition to the above drinks, you may add the following beverages:

- Hot water, honey, lemon and cayenne pepper

- Herbal teas

- Aloe vera (look for the fasting or detox formula)

- Noni Juice

CONSECRATION SHOPPING LIST

Please read all labels before purchasing. Do not purchase foods containing refined sugars, artificial sweeteners, excessive salt and/or additives. Please consult your doctor (especially those on medication) before you alter your diet or initiate a fast.

VEGETABLES

Avocados, Leeks, Carrots, Yams, Bean Sprouts, Cabbage, Broccoli, Radishes, Beets, Peppers, Cucumber, Watercress, Potatoes, Squashes, Plantain, Eggplant, Celery, Kohlrabi, Cauliflower, Zucchini, Peas, Turnips, Pumpkin, Brussels Sprouts, Onions, Sweet Potatoes, Parsnips, Artichokes, Asparagus, Tomatoes

SALAD/GREEN LEAFY VEGETABLES

Romaine Lettuce, Chives, Lamb's Lettuce, Curly Endive, Oak Leaf, Butter Head Lettuce, Boston Lettuce, Radicchio, Watercress, Coriander, Spinach, Swiss Chard, Kale, Spinach Beet, Mixed Swiss Chard, Collard Greens, Chicory

FRUIT

Apples, Tangerines, Apricots, Grapes, Blackberries, Cherries, Lemons, Cranberries, Strawberries, Grapefruit, Pears, Plums, Greengages, Guavas, Pineapples, Melons (eat alone), Kiwi Fruit, Peaches, Mangoes, Star Fruit, Limes, Papaya, Currents, Cranberries, Gooseberries

BREADS/CEREALS/GRAINS

Spelt, Barley, Sprouted Grains, Ezekiel Bread, Pumpernickel, Rye, Oat, Millet, Quinoa, Amaranth, Buckwheat, Wheat Germ, Brown Rice, Wild Rice, Basmati Rice

NUTS/SEEDS

Almond, Cashew, Pistachio, Walnut, Brazil, Filbert (Hazel Nut), Macadamia, Pecan, Pine Nut, Sunflower Seeds, Pumpkin Seeds, Sesame Seeds

HERBS/SPICES

Fresh Ginger, Garlic, Cilantro, Dill, Chives, Bay Leaves, Basil, Coriander, Oregano, Thyme, Parsley, Marjoram, Tarragon, Mint, Rosemary, Sage

LEGUMES/BEANS/SPROUTS

Adzuki Beans, Kidney Beans, Green Beans, Navy Beans, Pole Beans, String Beans, Lentils, Chickpeas, Red Beans, Mung Beans, Broad Beans, Yam Beans, Wax Beans, Black-Eyed Beans, Butter Beans, Cannelloni Beans, Lima Beans, Pinto Beans, Haricot Beans, Soy Beans (Edamame), Alfalfa Sprouts, Bean Sprouts, Broccoli Sprouts

DRIED FRUITS

Dates, Figs, Prunes, Raisins

DAIRY OPTIONS

Almond Milk, Rice Milk, Goat Cheese, Natural Yogurt

DRINK LIST

Purified Water, Herbal or Green Teas (including Yerba Mate and Rooibos), Fresh Vegetable Juices, Fresh Fruit Juices, Green Drinks, Noni Juice, Hot Water and Lemon

SWEETNERS

Honey, Agave, Molasses, Stevia (natural sweetener from the Stevia flower)

OTHER

Free-Roaming Hen Eggs, Sea Vegetables, Nori, Wakame, TVP (Texturized Vegetable Protein), Seitan, Tofu, Hummus, Veggie Cheese, Olive Oil, Agar, Safflower Oil, Sesame Oil, Apple Cider Vinegar, Natural Mayonnaise, Fish, Ryvita Crackers, Ghee, Miso, Tempeh, Natto, Tahini, Roasted Barley (Coffee alternative), Sesame Butter, Smart Balance, Shoyo, Postum (Coffee alternative), Chicory (Coffee alternative)

SEASONING/CONDIMENTS

Miso, Tamari, Soy Sauce, Vege-Sal, Braggs Liquid Aminos, Allspice, Cayenne Pepper, Cinnamon, Ginger, Cloves, Tofu Spreads, Mustard, Saffron, Sea Salt, Turmeric, Paprika, Balsamic Vinegar/Oil (makes a delicious salad dressing), Other Natural Herbs and Spices

SUPPLEMENTS

ChlorOxygen Enzymes (consume with every meal), Cell Food Probiotic (upon rising), Omega 3 Spirulina, CoQ10 Olive Leaf, Garlic Tabs Cayenne, Chromium Picolinate Colloidal Minerals and Selenium, A Good Multivitamin Grape Seed Extract

LIVER TONIC

Black Grapes

Fresh Garlic/Garlic Tablets

Pure Carrot/Beet/Celery Juice (3 times per week)

KIDNEY TONIC

Cranberry Tablet Supplement

Hot Water/Molasses/Braggs Apple Cider Vinegar

Hot Water/Lemon/Braggs Apple Cider Vinegar/Cayenne/Grade B Maple Syrup

FOODS TO AVOID

- Salt

- Refined Sugar

- Refined or Prepackaged Foods (frozen dinners or prepared dinners from a box)

- Wheat/Wheat Products (including refined breads)

- Most Snack Foods

- Dairy Products/Cow's Milk (full of steroids/growth hormones)

- Fried Foods

- Fast Foods

- Red Meats

- Processed Luncheon Meats

- Chicken

- Pork

- Shellfish

- Mushrooms (full of fungus)

- Oranges (too acidic)

- Peanuts

- Chocolates

- Baked Goods (cakes/cookies/pies)

- Candy

- Sodas

- Ocean Spray Juices (they are not all 100%)

- Carbonated Water

- Coffee

SAMPLE DAILY MEAL PLAN

Eat six times daily instead of three.

Take enzymes with each meal.

Drink herbal or green tea throughout the day.

UPON RISING

Drink Hot Water and Lemon

Take your Probiotic, Cell Food, and ChlorOxyen

A half hour later drink Noni Juice or other Green Drink

BREAKFAST OPTIONS (6:00 A.M.–9:00 A.M.)

Oatmeal or Rice Cereal and Fresh Fruit with Almond Milk

Poached or Hardboiled Eggs with Toast (see list of suggested breads)

Fresh Fruit with Natural Yogurt garnished with Raw Almonds or Walnuts

MID MORNING SNACK OPTIONS

Fresh Fruit

Rice Cake with Almond Butter

Dried Fruit & Nuts (no peanuts)

LUNCH OPTIONS (12:00 P.M.–2:00 P.M.)

Green Salad, Fish, Steamed Vegetables

Brown Rice and Beans or Lentils, Fresh Vegetables

Fresh Vegetable Salad, Baked Sweet Potato or Yam

Sardine Salad on Toast, Raw Vegetables

Broth-Based Soup (not creamy), Fresh Salad

MID AFTERNOON SNACK OPTIONS

Fresh Fruit

Vegetable Salad

Edamame

Nuts and Dried Fruit

Rice Cake

DINNER (5:00 P.M.–7:00P.M.)

Brown Rice with Steamed Vegetables and Green Salad

Tofu or Fish, Baked Yam, Fresh Vegetables

NIGHT SNACK

Melon

Warm Rice or Almond Milk

REFRESHING/INVIGORATING BEVERAGES

Lemon, Maple Syrup, and Pinch of Cayenne (see Master Cleanser recipe)

Herbal or Green Teas

BE SURE TO CONSUME THE FOLLOWING ON A DAILY BASIS:

- Hot water and lemon upon rising (alternate with Noni)

- Raw vegetables x3

- Water x8

- Fresh fruit x3

- Fresh green salad x3

- Whole grain x2

- Beans/seeds/nuts/grains x2

- Protein x3

- Kelp supplement x1

- Multivitamin (read label)

- Garlic tabs (read label)

- Probiotics x2

- Cell food x3

- Chloroxygen x2

- Olive leaf x3

- Coloidal minerals x2

- Cayenne x3

- Chromimum picolinate x2

- Flaxseed x3

- Noni x2

Upon rising/before retiring—alternate with hot water and lemon.

WHAT TO EXPECT

You may experience some of the following symptoms as the body rids itself of toxins:

- Fuzzy/coated tongue

- Headache

- Irritability

- Increase bowel movement

- Constipation

- Change in skin tone

- Nausea

- Breakouts

- Change in body scent

- Bad breath

DO'S FOR BODY MAINTENANCE

- Take cold showers/baths daily

- Dry skin brushing with loofah brush (exfoliates skin and increases circulation)

- Self massage

- Maintain peaceful environment

- Exercise (brisk walking outdoors)

- Steam baths/sauna (twice weekly)

- Bathe twice weekly in Epsom salts or baking soda (draws out impurities)

DO'S FOR SPIRITUAL MAINTENANCE

- Daily Scripture reading

- Prayer

- Journaling

- Personal devotions/meditations

Most importantly, throughout the fasting process, be reminded of the following benefits:

- Spiritual rejuvenation

- Vital energies are liberated from the laborious task of digestion and redirected to healing and repairing the body's tissues

- Mental alertness and centeredness

- Physical healing, emotional well-being

- Can be used as a preventive/curative measure for a chronic condition

- Alleviates chronic fatigue

- Increases energy, endurance, and longevity

- Regulates bowel movements and sleep patterns

MAKE A DECISION TO LEAD A HEALTHY LIFESTYLE

A decision to lead a healthy lifestyle requires a change of mindset and a commitment on your part.

Look at the statement of commitment below and check off the steps that you will take on the road to wellness and healthful living.

I will change my diet and lifestyle in the following ways:

- Eliminate red meat

- Eliminate dairy and fried foods

- Reduce salt, sugar, and alcohol

- Eliminate nicotine and caffeine

- Increase intake of beans and grains

- Increase intake of fruits and salads

- Increase intake of steamed, stir-fried, baked, and grilled vegetables

- Eliminate re-fried foods

- Substitute high fat, sugary, and salty snacks with healthy alternatives

- Detox at least twice a year

- Fast at least once a month

- Rid my life and environment of all waste and clutter

- Spend 30 minutes every day walking outdoors

- Invest quality time each day in something that brings me joy

- Show the people I love how much they mean to me daily

- Let the Lord know how much I appreciate all He's doing in my life

TAKE THE CREED

Read this creed aloud for the next 40 days. You will gain confidence and courage, and you will see marvelous things beginning to happen to you, in you, and around you. Dare to live the life of your dreams!

I have the courage and personal integrity to:

- Be myself

- Dream about a better life

- Wake up and live the life of my dreams

- Enjoy today and believe that tomorrow will be better than today

- Voice my opinions

- Pursue my goals

- Change my mind

- Break self-destructive activities, thoughts, and cycles of failure

- Set clear boundaries for myself and help others to respect them

- Change for the best

- Be my best

- Give my best

- Do my best

- Put my best foot forward

- Enjoy giving and receiving life

- Face and transform my fears with courage

- Seek and ask for support when I need it

- Spring free from the super-person trap

- Stop being all things to everyone

- Trust myself to know what is right for me

- Make my own decisions based on my perceptions of options

- Befriend myself

- Be kind to myself

- Be totally honest with myself

- Respect my vulnerabilities

- Heal old and current wounds

- Acquire new, good, and useful habits and eliminate the bad

- Complete unfinished business

- View my failures as life lessons

- Turn my losses into gain

- Realize that I have emotional and practical rights

- Honor my commitments

- Keep my promises

- Give myself credit for my accomplishments

- Love the little girl/boy in me

- Overcome my addictions and need for approval

- Grant myself permission to laugh out loud

- Live life out loud

- Play as hard as I can

- Dance like no one is watching

- Sing at the top of my voice

- Color outside of the lines

- Watch Mother Nature as she tucks the sun in for a good night's sleep and then turns the nightlights on for my enjoyment, security, and pleasure

- Witness the dawning of a new day as the sun rubs lingering sleepiness from its eyes

- Choose life over death

- Choose success over failure

- Live with an attitude of gratitude

- Quit being a trash receptacle and dumping bin

- Rid myself of toxic relationships

- Pursue and develop healthy and supportive relationships
- Renegotiate the terms of all relationships
- Nurture myself like I nurture others
- Take "me moments"
- Be alone without feeling lonely
- Demand that people give to me as much as I give them
- Manage my time
- Value the time that God has given me by using it wisely
- Demand others to value my time
- Be more objective about my feelings and subjective about my thoughts
- Detoxify all areas of my life
- Take an emotional enema when necessary
- Nurture others because I want to not because I have to
- Choose what is right for me
- Insist on being paid fairly for what I do
- Know when enough is enough
- Say "No" and mean it
- Put an end to toxic cycles
- Set limits and boundaries
- Say "Yes" only when I really mean it
- Have realistic expectations
- Take risks and accept change
- Live morally
- Conduct my affairs ethically
- Grow through change
- Grow through challenges
- Give others permissions to grow and be themselves
- Break glass ceilings
- Live beyond the limits

- Set new goals

- Savor the mystery of the Holy Spirit

- Pray and expect an exceptional and favorable outcome

- Meditate in order to un-clutter my mind

- Wave good-bye to guilt, self-doubt, rejection, and insecurity

- De-weed the flower bed of my thought life

- Treat myself with respect and teach others to do the same

- Fill my own cup first, and then refresh others from the overflow

- Demand excellence from others and myself

- Plan for the future but live in the present

- Value my insight, intelligence, and wisdom

- Know that I am loveable

- Celebrate the differences in others

- Make forgiveness a priority

- Accept myself just as I am now and forever

- Live within my means

- Manifest His divinity

- Breathe beyond innate fears by living in the realm of faith

- Embrace His Spirit, which is stronger and wiser than mine

- Prosper beyond my imagination

- Give more than I receive

- Give to those who can never return the favor

- Love unconditionally

- Live consciously

Therefore, I will:

- Give God the time He needs

- Give my mind the order and peace it needs

- Give my life the discipline it needs

- Give my spirit the freedom it needs

- Give my soul the love it needs

- Give my body the nourishment and exercise it needs

- Give my voice the platform it needs

- Take a stand for what I believe

- Give myself the love and attention I need

- Pursue my dreams and accomplish my goals

- Pursue my purpose and maximize my potential

- Stand on truth and take a stand for truth

- Positively impact my generation

- Positively influence a system and/or an institution

- Live, learn, love, serve, and then leave a legacy

I am on a collision course with destiny:

- I am at the Intersection of Truth; the Avenue of Opportunity; the Boulevard of Passion; and on a Street named Courage.

- All lights are green. I choose to proceed.

- Today, I crash and walk away with purpose, success, and nobility.

Today and always:

- I alone accept and own full and total responsibility for being my genuine and true self.

Therefore,

- I vow to live authentically, to grow and care for my best and nobler self that I may reflect the shimmer of God's glory and divinity.

- Today, I shall be blessed with all good things.

- My day shall be good.

- I will have good success.

- My joy, peace, prosperity, and success shall be as abundant as the stars at night.

- Friendship, favor, affluence, influence, health, happiness, support, beauty, and abundant living shall be my constant companion.

- I am unconditionally loved, celebrated, revered, appreciated, and honored beyond measure and human comprehension.

- I make a difference in this world.

- This is my contract with myself.

- And today, I give myself permission to push until I succeed.

_____

Signed

_____

Dated

ASK YOURSELF THESE 24 QUESTIONS:

1. Who am I outside of the roles I play?

2. What are my long-term goals?

3. What should I be doing with my life right now?

4. What are my strengths?

5. What are my weaknesses?

6. What direction will my life go if I continue doing what I'm doing?

7. How can I be sure I am in the right place, doing the right thing?

8. What is my purpose?

9. Who should I be partnering with?

10. What resources are available for me to accomplish my goals?

11. Do I like the person I've become?

12. What do I really want to achieve in this lifetime?

13. What brings me my greatest joy?

14. What am I really passionate about?

15. What frustrates me most or makes me sad?

16. If I could do something other than what I am doing now, what would that be?

17. If I could live somewhere else, where would that be?

18. Do these things that I do and am involved with make me feel good and happy?

19. Are my relationships mutually beneficial and symbiotic?

20. Is there room for improvement in my relationships?

21. What have I accomplished so far with my life? Is it enough?

22. If I could do one thing different, what would it be?

23. After my death, will future generations know that I lived?

24. How do I want people to remember me?

Empowering You for Life!

LOOKING FOR MORE?

Please visit me online at www.trimminternational.com for more tools and resources to nurture the life of your soul. If you want to take part in the Soul Fast Movement, please go to www.soulfast.com to find out how you can get involved, enroll in our ongoing programs, or participate in a guided, interactive *40 Day Soul Fast*. Two times per year, I host an eight-week program when I personally coach you through each of the 40 Characteristics via my weekly empowerment broadcast, daily video blog, and downloadable phone app. There you also will find a free "Dynamic Life Questionnaire," an online community where you can always continue the conversation, as well as other soul-enhancing resources.

Let's do life together! Join with me as I endeavor to heal the world by healing the souls of individuals—empowering them to impact their communities and nations all across the globe. Every soul is significant and influences the world in countless ways. Never doubt that what you do *does* make a difference! You could be the answer someone else is looking for. Don't wait another day to step up to the plate—the world's next homerun could be depending on you to make the pitch. Pitch life. Pitch healing!

I value you and what you bring to the game. Let's make a difference and bring healing wherever we are. Let's make this life a winning proposition for all. For more about soul healing and empowerment, please visit me online. Join the soul healing movement or create your own. If you are interested in pioneering the unexplored frontiers of your own destiny, enroll in my signature *Executive Life Coaching* personal and professional achievement program, or register to attend a Trimm University intensive school of leadership, prayer, or ministry.

As always, I look forward to empowering you for life!

Dr. Cindy Trimm

The Life Empowerment Program provides you with 365-days of life strategies designed to unlock your fullest potential. As your empowerment mentor, each day Dr. Cindy Trimm will share key principles and insights that will take you where you want to be a year from today. Imagine where your life could be this time next year! By making just a few adjustments, taking deliberate action with a little focused effort and conscious intention, you will make quantum progress. This is what this program is all about.

Receive a daily e-video teaching packed with practical life principles that will equip you to:

- Grow emotionally, professionally, relationally

- Discover and unlock the seed of greatness hidden with you

- Dramatically increase your ability to fulfill any goal or desire

- Add meaning to what you're doing

- Expand your influence with others

- Learn what it takes to win at life

- Put the "wow" back into daily living

Sign up today at www.yourlifeempowerment.com or call us at 866-444-7258.

SOON TO BE RELEASED:

Heal Your Soul, Heal Our World

Reclaim Your Soul

Reclaim Your Health

The Creed

The Quest

The Journey

OTHER RESOURCES FOR SPIRITUAL ENRICHMENT FROM DR. TRIMM INCLUDE:

The Prayer Warrior's Way

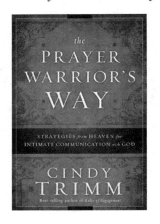

The Rules of Engagement

Commanding Your Morning

When Kingdoms Clash

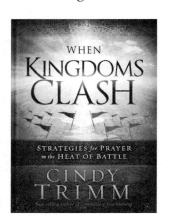

The Art of War for Spiritual Battle

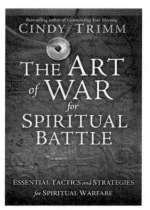

ABOUT DR. CINDY TRIMM

A best-selling author, high-impact teacher, and former senator, Dr. Trimm is a sought-after empowerment specialist, revolutionary thinker, and transformational leader. She has earned a distinguished reputation as a catalyst for change and voice of hope to the nations.

Listed among *Ebony* magazine's *Power 100* as the "top 100 doers and influencers in the world today," Dr. Trimm is a featured speaker on some of the world's largest platforms, a frequent guest on Christian broadcasting's most popular TV and radio shows, and continually tops the Black Christian News Network and Black Christian Book Company's National Bestsellers List.

Dr. Trimm combines her wealth of leadership expertise with her depth of spiritual understanding to reveal life-transforming messages that empower and inspire. Seasoned with humor, compassion, revelatory insight, and personal candor, Dr. Trimm opens minds and touches hearts with biblically-based principles of inner healing and personal empowerment.

Pulling on her background in government, education, psychology, and human development, Dr. Trimm translates hard-hitting spiritual insights into everyday language that empower individuals to transform their lives—helping change the path people take in search of meaning, dignity, purpose, and hope.

In the right hands, This Book will Change Lives!

Most of the people who need this message will not be looking for this book. To change their lives, you need to put a copy of this book in their hands.

> *But others (seeds) fell into good ground, and brought forth fruit, some a hundred-fold, some sixty-fold, some thirty-fold* (Matthew 13:8).

Our ministry is constantly seeking methods to find the good ground, the people who need this anointed message to change their lives. Will you help us reach these people?

> *Remember this—a farmer who plants only a few seeds will get a small crop. But the one who plants generously will get a generous crop* (2 Corinthians 9:6).

EXTEND THIS MINISTRY BY SOWING
3 BOOKS, 5 BOOKS, 10 BOOKS, **OR MORE TODAY,**
AND BECOME A LIFE CHANGER!

Thank you,

Don Nori Sr., Founder
Destiny Image
Since 1982